TREACHERY ON THE TWISTED RIVER

DON RICHARDSON

PEACE CHILD, ADAPTED FOR YOUNG READERS
BY KAREN ROBERTSON

Treachery on the Twisted River
by Don Richardson
adapted by Karen Robertson

© 2020, Pioneers-USA

This book has been adapted from *Peace Child,* by Don Richardson, with permission from Baker Publishing Group and the Richardson family.

Cover illustration: Katarzyna Surman
Cover design: Danny Anan
Photos: the Richardson family
Editorial: Marti Wade, Karen Robertson, Maxine McDonald

ISBN: 978-1-7352345-2-6

CONTENTS

NOTE TO PARENTS

Since its publication in 1974, *Peace Child*, by Don Richardson, has become a missions classic, with more than 400,000 copies in print in twenty-five languages. The story of the gospel's transformation of an isolated tribe of headhunters in the swamps of Indonesia has inspired many young people to consider the risks and rewards of giving their lives to the cause of global missions.

That being said, the book candidly depicts the violence and despair that characterized Sawi culture when the Richardsons arrived. As such, many parents may be hesitant to allow their children to read the book—or may not wish to read it aloud to them.

That was the concern that motivated Karen Robertson to adapt *Peace Child* for younger audiences, editing the book both for length and content. *Treachery on the Twisted River* does not attempt to remove all violence from *Peace Child*, but it also does not dwell on it, instead depicting it in a way that may be more understandable to children ages twelve and older.

Each child is different, and the book may be suitable reading for some children younger than twelve, and there may be those older who are too sensitive to enjoy the book. We trust parents to decide what is appropriate for each of their children.

More than a tale of headhunters and cannibals, *Treachery on the Twisted River* is a story that combines high adventure, familial love, humor and the timeless truth of God's passion to reconcile to Himself those in darkness.

We hope this book inspires family conversations about God's love for people—whether they live in the jungles of Southeast Asia or are next-door neighbors. Perhaps a child will feel the tug of the Holy Spirit calling them to imagine how He may use them to bring peace to a broken world.

FOREWORD

The true stories in this book took place in the southwest portion of the world's second-largest island, New Guinea, in the late 1950s and early 1960s. Rugged, snow-capped mountains cover much of the interior of the island. The low swamplands, where the Sawi live, are hot, humid, and covered with nearly impassable jungle.

New Guinea lies just south of the equator, near Australia's northeast coast. The Netherlands controlled the western half of the island up until the early 1960s. At that time they gave control of the area—currently called Papua—to the United Nations, who then gave it to the Indonesian government. Most New Guineans are Melanesians—a Pacific people with darker skin and textured hair.

The Sawi, and other tribes of the area, knew how to take advantage of the jungle's bounty. Sago flour provided the main part of their diet, along with wild pigs, tropical fruit, and beetle grubs. On occasion the Sawi diet also included human flesh.

At the beginning of the book, you'll discover how the Sawi lived in fear before they heard about God's love—fear of neighbors, fear of evil spirits, even fear of "friends" who might be plotting treachery.

Be forewarned that the Sawi, before learning about God, acted savagely and brutally. You may be horrified by their violence and some of their customs. But know that change—change for the better—will come in a few short chapters.

Are you ready for this adventure? Read on!

CHARACTER AND LOCATION GUIDE

The five tribes of southwest Papua

Sawi, Kayagar, Atohwaem, Asmat, and Auyu

MAIN CHARACTERS

Mauro village (Sawi Tribe)

Yae and his wife Anai

Haenam village (Sawi Tribe)

Kauwan

Giriman

Paha, his wife Syado, and their son Mani

Maum

Kani

Mavu

Sauni

Mahor

Wario

Kamur village (Sawi Tribe)

Nair

Kigo

Numu

Ari

Sinau

Atae

Kaiyo, his wife Wumi, and their son Biakadon
Miri

Wasohwi village (Sawi Tribe)
Fusuman

Yohwi village (Atohwaem Tribe)
Hadi
Yadai

Kayagar Tribe
Hurip
Hedip

Foreign missionaries
Don and Carol Richardson and their sons Stephen,
    Shannon, and Paul and their daughter Valerie
John and Glenna McCain

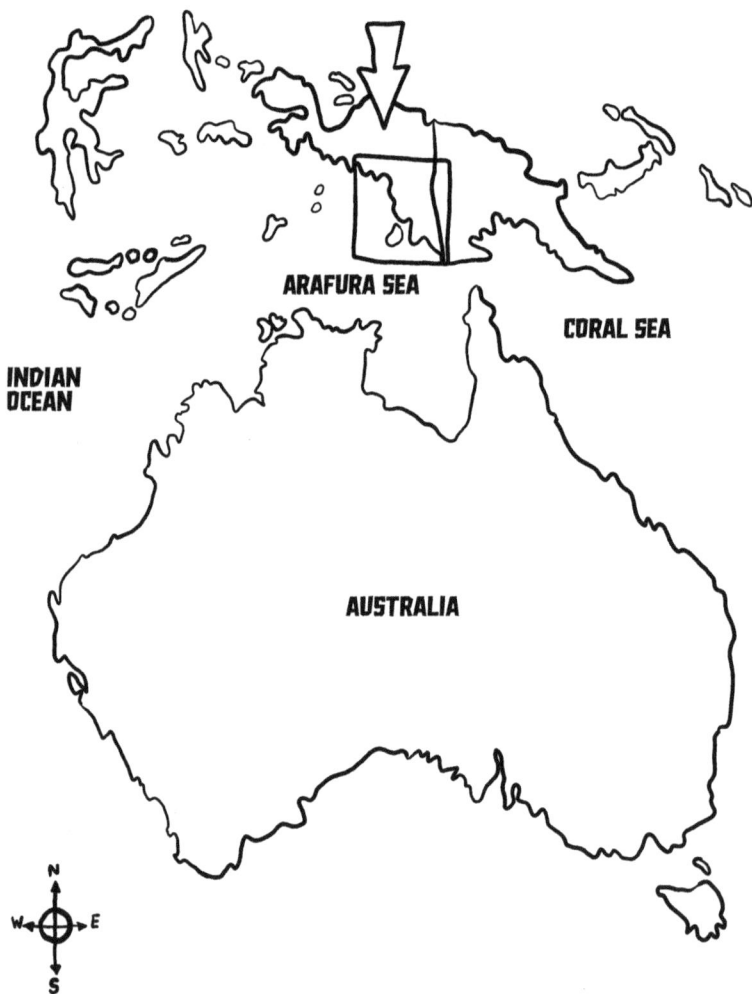

MAP NO. 1

PAPUA, INDONESIA
FORMERLY NETHERLANDS NEW GUINEA

ARAFURA SEA

CORAL SEA

INDIAN
OCEAN

AUSTRALIA

N
W ⊕ E
S

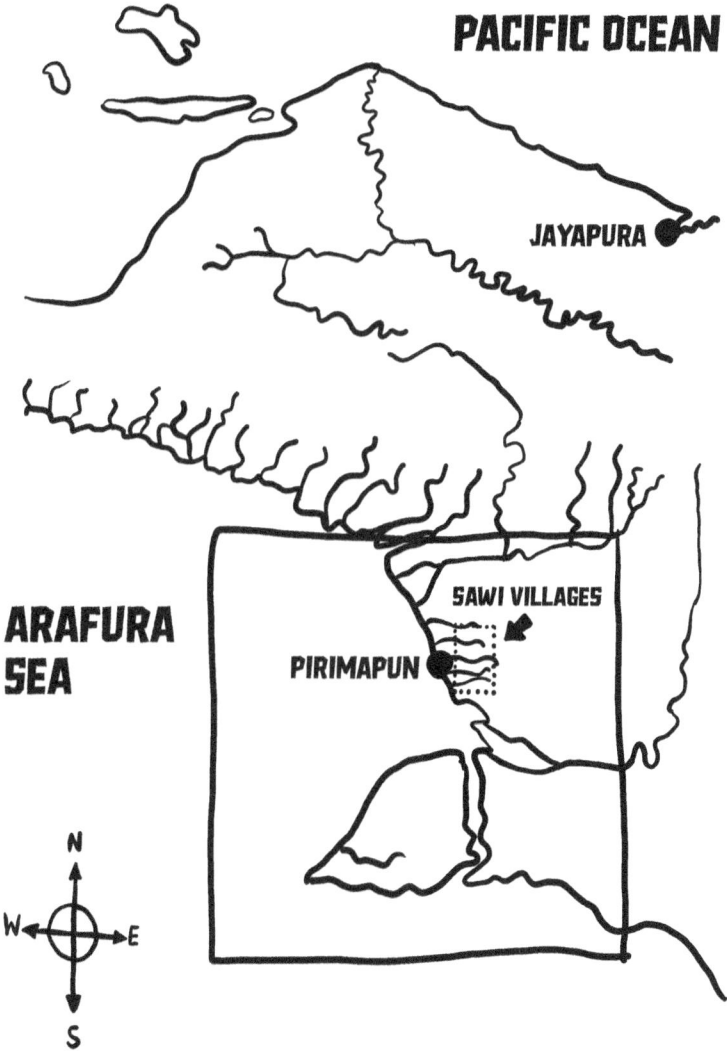

MAP NO. 2
SAWI REGION OF PAPUA

PACIFIC OCEAN

JAYAPURA

SAWI VILLAGES

ARAFURA
SEA

PIRIMAPUN

N
W E
S

MAP NO. 3
APPROXIMATE LOCATION
OF SAWI VILLAGES IN 1962

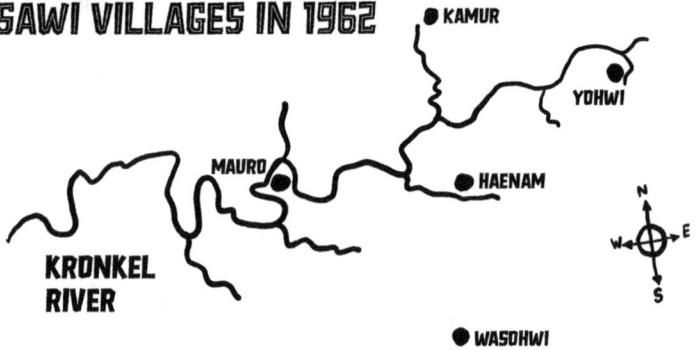

● KAMUR

● YOHWI

MAURO
●

● HAENAM

**KRONKEL
RIVER**

N
W ● E
S

● WASOHWI

CHAPTER 1

SEEKING PEACE ON THE TWISTED RIVER

Yae did not know it was his last day to walk the earth. He smiled in anticipation of his trip up the murky Kronkel River, named with the Dutch word for *twisted*.

The Kronkel did, indeed, twist through the swamps of southwest New Guinea. Five tribes lived, fought, and died among its coils: Sawi, Kayagar, Atohwaem, Asmat, and Auyu. Battles had raged for generations between tribes and between villages within each tribe. Yae was about to travel upstream to build an alliance with another Sawi village. The peace he sought would end only in death.

***

Just after dawn, Yae peered through the floorboards of his tree-house forty feet above the Kronkel's dark surface. Decaying leaves drifted downstream beneath him. The changing tide in the distant

Arafura Sea would soon push the river's black water back into the swamp. In a few minutes the leaves would pause, turn, and retreat upstream the way they had come.

A Sawi man paddles his dugout on the Kronkel.

Yae's wife, Anai[1], sat on the floor making sago-flour cakes. Their newborn baby slept peacefully in the corner while their two-year-old son played happily with his only toy—his grandfather's skull. It had been rubbed shiny by years of play. Yae and Anai believed the skull might keep away evil spirits. To the toddler it was just a toy.

---

1. Anai's name was really Kautap. It has been changed here to avoid confusion with other characters.

"The tide is turning. Cook my sago now," Yae ordered.

While Anai wrapped the sago paste in leaves to place in the hot coals, Yae put on his ornaments. First came a grass skirt, worn only by men who had killed an enemy in battle. Yae had killed five men and cut off the heads of three of them. Bracelets of wild boar tusks around his left elbow announced that fact to those who understood the code.

Next, Yae wrapped himself with a six-foot-long necklace of animal teeth, one tooth from each beast he had killed—wild pig, crocodile, dog, or marsupial. He fit bands of woven palm stems above and below the muscles on each bicep and just below his knees. Yae placed a six-inch-long hollow bone carved from a pig's thigh into his pierced nose. He left behind his feather plumes, marsupial-fur headband, and body paint. This was, after all, a visit to work on peace, not an all-night dance.

Anai handed the cooked sago to Yae. He ate half, placing the remainder in his food bag along with some pork Anai had smoked. He pulled his six-foot-long bow out of the overhead weapon rack and chose a number of barbed arrows. Finally, he took his paddle-spear with a sharp cassowary talon fixed at one end.

"Why do you go so often to Haenam village?" Anai complained as Yae began to climb down from the treehouse. "Doesn't your skin feel uneasy?" She meant, *Aren't you uncomfortable or nervous?*

"If I had no friends there," Yae paused on the ladder, "then I wouldn't go. There is no need to worry." He continued his downward climb confidently, not once touching his hands to the rungs.

Yae stepped off the final rung and walked to his dugout canoe. On the way he passed by the six other treehouses that made up Mauro village. All measured about forty feet long and balanced in the treetops at a height between thirty and fifty feet.

"I'm going to invite my friends in Haenam to come to our dance," he told a friend at the water's edge.

"Good luck," the friend called back as he stepped onto the stern of his dugout canoe. His three wives stood near the bow of the thirty-foot canoe. They raised their paddles together as they headed out to a sago swamp.

Yae stepped into his own canoe and began paddling swiftly upstream, aided by the change in the current. Cockatoos screamed in alarm at his approach, waking up a crocodile which slid lazily into the water. As he paddled, Yae reflected on the events that had made him the messenger between his village and Haenam.

***

Seven months earlier Yae had stumbled upon a hunting party from the enemy village of Haenam. He had crouched down, reaching for his spear.

"*Konahari!* Hello! Don't take your weapons! You are Yae, and we are related," one member of the Haenam group called.

Yae picked up his bow just in case, but was careful not to put an arrow to the string. "What is your name?" he demanded.

"I am Kauwan, the youngest son of your mother's stepfather," came the reply.

After more assurances of goodwill, Kauwan gave Yae an unexpected invitation to become a messenger between Mauro and Haenam—someone who would work to unite the two unfriendly Sawi villages against a common enemy, the Kayagar tribe. Kauwan promised to protect Yae's life with his own if he would agree to facilitate the negotiations. The other men vowed they, too, would guarantee his safety.

Yae felt tempted by the offer. He knew that the Kayagar had caused many problems lately in the jungle. If the people of Haenam and Mauro worked together, it would benefit them both. Yae would become very important in the eyes of the other villagers. Men would want to give him their daughters in marriage—perhaps he could reach the Sawi goal of having five wives!

Yae had two wives, but one had died—leaving only Anai. He wanted another wife and this seemed to be a way to secure one, *if* he could trust Kauwan.

Kauwan certainly seemed sincere. He even cut off some of his hair and gave it to Yae—a sign of friendly intentions.

And yet... many people in Haenam held grudges against Mauro. Could Kauwan and his friends *really* protect him? Kauwan wore four boar-tusk bracelets for four heads he had taken. He was brave. But was he trustworthy?

Yae had to decide. If he refused Kauwan's request, someone else might get the honor. If he accepted, he might walk into a trap and be killed!

Yae's heart beat wildly—he had a chance to become a hero! Or—he would be murdered.

"Yes," Yae chose boldly, "I will come!"

***

Having given his word, Yae had to follow through or others would call him a coward. He had to negotiate with the people of Haenam on behalf of Mauro. Now here he was, setting out on his eleventh visit—almost ready to finalize the peace agreement he had been working for. And *he* would get the credit for it!

At least, Yae *thought* an agreement was coming that would bring him honor and respect. He thought wrong.

CHAPTER 2

FATTENED WITH FRIENDSHIP

Yae paddled through the morning, periodically reaching down to scoop some water into his hand. He tossed each scoop up, catching it mid-air with his mouth. All Sawi knew that this was the only way to drink water. Any other way could be dangerous. Evil spirits lived in the river. They might enter the body if one drank from it directly.

Up ahead, hanging in the bushes, Yae spotted a decorated skull. Red seeds in black tree sap filled the eye sockets and feathers hung from each ear hole. The marker showed which stream led to Haenam village, where Yae was soon to gain fame and power. He had convinced himself of it.

Kauwan greeted Yae just as he had each time before. "This is my friend!" he proclaimed to the other Haenam villagers. "He is welcome here! Who is there who might want to harm him? He will not be harmed! My hand is strong!"

Yae and Kauwan walked to the manhouse. Others joined them, forming a circle around Yae. The men laughed and ate, enjoying the chance to visit and share stories.

"I have come to invite you to a party in my village," Yae said, smiling.

"You are an old friend, Yae," the warrior Giriman stated. "I will come to your party!" Paha[2], another villager, agreed. Soon twelve men accepted the invitation. They handed Yae a length of string and asked him to tie one knot in it for each day they must count off before coming to the party.

Delighted, Yae bent over the rope, eyes down. Paha looked at Giriman and raised his eyebrows slightly. Giriman passed the signal on to Maum, who passed it to Kani and so it went around the circle. Soon all the men had noticed the signal.

Paha's hand slid under the edge of his grass mat and his fingers wrapped around a long, needle-sharp bone dagger. Giriman, Kani, Maum, and the other men from Haenam slowly stood, pretending to stretch. As they lifted their hands, they pulled out barbed spears from the overhead weapons rack. Wicked grins split their faces.

---

2. Paha's name was really Mahaen. It has been changed here to avoid confusion with other characters.

Yae, completely unaware of the danger, continued tying knots. Kauwan chatted on with him as if nothing bad were happening. The armed men inched closer.

Slowly, like fog stealing over the swamp, Yae felt a chill enter his heart. It felt darker around him, and quieter. His skin began to crawl, but he forced himself to look up hopefully. Weapons and glimmering eyes greeted him. The men of Haenam had waited seven long months for the moment when Yae would realize that he had been treated kindly so that he could be betrayed. They had fattened him with friendship for the slaughter.

The Haenam warriors watched with glee as Yae's happy face filled with terror. For months afterward they would sit around telling and retelling every detail of Yae's murder—how his eyes grew wide, how his lips trembled in fear, how sweat broke out all over his body. They would rock back and forth with laughter. What a perfect betrayal! They'd done it!

"*Tuwi asonai makaerin!*" Giriman hissed, "We have fattened you with friendship for the slaughter!"

Those three Sawi words revealed one of the deepest parts of the Sawi culture—a love of treachery. Yae realized that the men of Haenam had meant to kill him from the beginning, but they were sure he would come back again and again. If they had killed him the day they met him on the river, that would have been just ordinary murder. Anyone could do that! But to keep up a pretend friendship for months, then finish the friendship with death—ah! That was what made them heroes in Sawi history!

Yae frantically searched for a way out. *Why did I come to Haenam in the first place? Because I trusted Kauwan. Kauwan? Where was Kauwan now? Perhaps he will still save me!*

"Kauwan!" Yae gasped, "Protect me!"

Kauwan replied calmly, sarcastically, "I kept telling them this was bad, that you are my friend, and they shouldn't do this to you. But Maum promised to give me his daughter in marriage if I kept silent. Too bad, *friend*. I'm not going to help you."

Yae screamed, "Stand by your promise, Kauwan!"

He tried to rise, but Maum's spear struck him in the side. Yae stumbled to one knee, trying vainly to pull out the barbed weapon. "Help me, Kauwan! Have mercy!"

Kauwan turned away and shrugged, "You should have given me a peace child. Then I would have protected you."

Yae thought of Anai and their newborn baby back in the treehouse at Mauro. The baby could have saved him! But now it was too late.

A stone axe hit him from behind, below the shoulder blade. Yae pitched forward, gasping in pain. A second spear pierced through the calf of one of his legs. Rage rushed through him like windswept fire. Yae lurched to his feet, blood streaming from his wounds. His tormentors laughed and continued attacking him.

Yae fell forward again, his face looking down through a gap in the floorboards. Chickens, fifteen feet below, cocked their heads at the noise. Yae remembered his paddle-spear stuck in the river mud. If only he could get down to the river! Then he could use the spear end to take at least one life in exchange for his own.

Head first, Yae slipped down through the opening, but the spear in his leg caught on the floor poles, leaving him hanging upside down. He twisted in the air as his betrayers ran out of the man-house, arrows fitted in their bows. Women and children came running—delighted with this rare chance to help kill a victim.

Children shot their small arrows into Yae. Women clubbed him with sago-digging sticks. Dogs raced in and out of the chaos, yelping when stepped on.

The killing frenzy raged on until Yae stopped moving. Someone wrenched the spear out of the floor poles and Yae's body fell to the ground. Warriors danced wildly around the corpse, boasting about their part in the murder.

Maum approached the corpse. He had purchased Kauwan's silence, so he had the right to cut off Yae's head. Maum chopped away with his stone axe until the dull blade severed the tendons and vertebrae. He gave Yae's jawbone as a prize to one of the women. She was thrilled with the honor and looked adoringly at Maum.

The men of Haenam carried Yae's corpse back into the man-house and placed it on banana leaves, ready to be cut up. Three of them held sharpened bamboo knives. Onlookers shouted out their claims to different parts of Yae's body. Then the butchering began.

Women danced about, keeping time to a beat pounded on lizard-skin drumheads glued on with human blood. Those who had already eaten human flesh teased those who hadn't, assuring them that people tasted just like pork or cassowary.

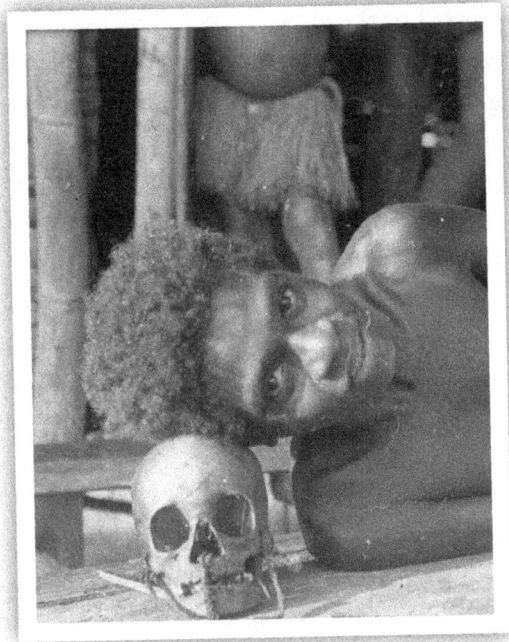

A human skull is used as a convenient pillow.

"Of course I will eat it!" some first-time cannibals boasted.

"Why would anyone want to eat that?" others giggled.

Eventually each of them would taste human flesh, overcoming the dread they felt. When a Sawi became a cannibal for the first time, it seemed to him (or her) that his eyes were opened to know both good and evil.

After the body had been cut up and set on grills to sizzle over cooking fires, Maum took Yae's head. He pulled out the brain and placed pieces of it on leaves and platters to be eaten with the cooked meat.

***

The news of Yae's death stunned Anai. She shaved her head, climbed down wailing from the treehouse, and threw herself into the riverbank mud. Then she hurled Yae's stone axe into the river so his spirit might use it in the world of the dead. Relatives killed a jungle pig Yae had caught, tamed, and raised for the planned party with Haenam so that it, too, might go with his spirit.

All of Mauro village mourned Yae's death. Treehouses swayed as villagers stamped from one end to the other in their grief. No drum sounded for three months, out of respect for Yae.

Anai expressed her grief through the words of a poem that she moaned over and over, tears flowing down her cheeks:

Oh who will deal with the children of treachery?
Oh who will overcome those who use friendship
    to fatten their victims?
Oh what will it take to make them cease?

While Anai mourned, Yae's relatives plotted against Haenam. Revenge was the only known choice. How else could they justify Yae's death?

Maum—the main plotter in Yae's murder—eventually heard about Anai's poem. He smiled as others repeated her words to him.

"Who indeed will overcome us?" he asked. He stretched out to take a nap. As he settled on his grass mat, Yae's skull rolled against him. Maum placed it under his head as a pillow and fell asleep.

CHAPTER 3

SHADOW OF THE TUANS

The Sawi villages on the Kronkel River continued to fear and fight one another. Haenam sought help from two other Sawi-speaking villages in order to take care of their problems with the neighboring Kayagar tribe. Mauro banded together with several other villages so they could fight against the Asmat near the mouth of the Kronkel River. Fighting broke out periodically, followed by times of tentative peace.

Mauro villagers still wanted to avenge Yae's death. They convinced another Sawi village, which was at peace with Haenam, to invite a group of Haenam warriors to an all-night dance. The plan worked; nine Haenam men went to the party, never dreaming men from Mauro might also come. Near dawn, at the end of the dance, Mauro warriors raced into the village and attacked the visitors from Haenam.

Five of the nine Haenam party-goers managed to escape, leaving bright trails of blood behind them. Kani, who had been part of the group that betrayed Yae, survived a spear wound to the back. Kani's older brother was not so lucky. Mauro men butchered and ate him and three of his friends.

Neither Mauro nor Haenam could be truly satisfied by bloodshed. Neither had any hope of real peace.

***

When interludes between fighting allowed tribes to trade and socialize, the Sawi noticed their Kayagar and Asmat neighbors using a new word. They spoke excitedly about something or someone called a *Tuan*. Only a few Sawi could make sense of the foreign languages, so it was very difficult to figure out what a *Tuan* was.

It seemed that Tuans were very large beings.

How frightening!

They were also known to be friendly, overall.

This was good news!

However, some of them had weapons that could spurt out fire and make a sound like thunder.

Even brave warriors trembled at this news!

They didn't like head-hunting or cannibalism.

Good! The Kayagar and Asmat needed to hear that. Perhaps they would stop killing the Sawi!

Tuan skin looked as white as sago flour…

How ugly they must be!

…and it felt very cool to the touch.

Could it be that they were not human at all?

They had straight or wavy hair and covered themselves with strange skins so you could hardly see the person.

How difficult it must be to know them as they really are!

No female Tuan had ever been seen, but some sources claimed that a few did exist.

They must have to fight fiercely for wives if there are so few women!

Tuans brought strange objects to trade. They had axes to cut down trees, machetes to slash through bushes, and knives to butcher meat. Tiny sticks could start a fire. Razors shaved whiskers much better than bamboo knives. Fishhooks and fish line let you catch fish in the main rivers instead of waiting by smaller tributaries until the water dropped low enough to spear fish or shoot them with arrows.

Mirrors showed your soul much more clearly than the surface of quiet swamp water. Salt made food much tastier. Tuans had soap that removed dirt and even skin-grease! The Tuans also had powers that prevented fevers and healed sores much better than Sawi witchcraft could.

The Sawi couldn't decide if they wanted to meet a Tuan or not. Yes, the goods they had seemed wonderful... but what if something bad happened in the spirit world because of the Tuans?

Sawi ancestors had established a precarious agreement with the demon spirits they believed lived throughout the jungle. "The spirits have accepted our skin-grease in their rivers," they claimed. True, sometimes horrible illnesses came and destroyed entire villages, but the spirits sent them far enough apart that the communities survived.

What would happen if a Tuan put his skin-grease into the river? Would the spirits take out their anger on the Sawi? Were the Tuans a new sort of spirit they would have to serve? How could the Sawi survive if they had to worry about spirits, other villages, other tribes, *and* Tuans?

Nothing in Sawi legends gave answers to these completely new and very frightening questions. What should they do? No one knew.

***

One day a canoe loaded with men from the Kayagar tribe came down the river to Haenam with an Atohwaem warrior named Hadi. Hadi spoke three languages: Atohwaem, Kayagar, and Sawi.

His village, Yohwi, had a close relationship with Haenam, and Hadi traveled back and forth frequently.

"These men have something very special to show you!" Hadi exclaimed in Sawi.

Haenam warriors slowly came out of their houses as Hadi leaped ashore. Hurip, a Kayagar, bent down and picked up a strange object. His eyes laughed at the astonished Sawi faces as he proclaimed the object's name.

Hadi translated. "This is a steel axe!"

The Sawi stared at the object with wonder. The axe blade measured as long as a man's hand. It was shiny and wide at one end; a wooden handle fit into a thick ring at the other.

Hadi pointed to a small tree and urged Hurip to show what the strange object could do. Hurip walked to the tree, raised the axe over his shoulder, and struck a blow deep into the trunk.

Hadi chuckled as the Sawi jumped at the strange-sounding crack of steel on wood. Hurip jerked out the blade and with three more blows sent the tree toppling over. Four blows! It would have taken over forty blows with a stone axe! Cheers and shouts of amazement rose up from the spectators.

Hadi and Hurip went up to the manhouse. The Sawi passed the axe from one to another, marveling that something so light and thin could cut down a tree without breaking.

Hurip smiled at their childlike wonder. "I traded my child to another Kayagar to get this axe," he boasted. "There is a Tuan living in Araray village."

"Hurip," Kani asked, "why did that Tuan come to live in Araray?"

When Hadi translated the question, Hurip shrugged his shoulders. "You must think the Tuans are like us!" he exclaimed. "If one of us moves to a certain place, you can know it is because he has much unharvested sago there, or because he wants to live where his father used to live. But the Tuans don't like sago. They don't seem to have any enemies. They come where they want, go where they want, and stay where they want! No one knows what they will do or why. All we know is wherever they go, their canoes are filled with axes like this one."

The Sawi whistled in wonder, but Kani persisted. "If a Tuan were to come here, what would happen to us?"

Hadi translated Hurip's reply. "You Sawi still cut off heads and eat human flesh. If a Tuan comes here, you'll have to stop that sort of thing. If you don't, he'll shoot fire at you. You'll have to work instead. Then the Tuan will give you lots of axes, machetes, and knives."

Some Sawi whistled in amazement. Others became quiet at the thought of never eating human flesh again, never cutting off heads, and possibly being burned with fire.

Kani did not whistle. They had not yet taken revenge against Mauro for wounding him and killing his brother. If the people of

Haenam were going to get revenge, it had to happen soon, before any Tuans came. Kani decided it was time to *tuwi asonai man*—to fatten pigs for slaughter. Other ways of getting revenge had failed. They would have to use false friendship again.

CHAPTER 4

THE TUANS ARE COMING

Kani's plan for revenge was drenched with trickery, yet he knew it would fail if his friends didn't join him. He had carefully plotted how to share the scheme. Kani smiled with nervous anticipation as he saw Maum, Mavu, and Sauni arrive in a canoe. Now he would share his idea.

Kani greeted his friends by the river, but suddenly the smile froze on his face. Somewhere, far away, a strange sound began to pulse, growing louder by the second, beating like a gigantic heart.

Kani, Maum, Mavu, and Sauni frantically searched their memories. They had never heard anything like this before! Not ocean breakers, not a distant thunderstorm forming, nothing man-made or from an animal. The sound must come from something supernatural!

Terror swelled each heart and Maum remembered the warning Hurip had given about the Tuans—"They will shoot fire at you!"

"Run!" Maum screamed.

Women and children frantically passed babies, grass mats, and stone-age tools out of treehouses. Rapid evacuations from war parties happened frequently. This time, though, the men fled with the women and children, carrying weapons in addition to grass mats.

Kani, Maum, and a few other men decided to hide in the bushes near the riverbank to catch a glimpse of the approaching monster.

The sound grew, making the swamp itself tremble. It seemed to come from all sides, bouncing around the forest. Slowly, they noticed that the sound seemed focused in the west. Then it moved south, which meant that it was following the bends of the Kronkel! One more turn and it would reach them!

Kani fitted an arrow into his bow, though he doubted he could release it at the doom coming toward him. All at once the sound grew so loud that his skin felt cold and the hair on his neck stood out straight.

Waves larger than any Kani had ever seen appeared on the Kronkel, shaking and tossing the sturdy *ahos* trees. The monster creating those waves would soon sweep into view.

***

Two covered riverboats churned around yet another bend of the Kronkel. Their diesel engines throbbed together, drowning out other sounds. Dutch officials had come to explore the area. They were searching for hidden villages and a place to build a government outpost to begin to tame this wild jungle area. They had been traveling for several days.

For protection against enemies and flooding rivers, Sawi homes were built on poles high above the ground.

The Sawi were semi-nomadic. They chose not to fix their tree-houses. Whenever the poles supporting them began to rot, they simply packed up their goods, moved to another spot, and built new homes. Such frequent moves made them very difficult to find.

Recently, however, both Kani's village of Haenam and another Sawi village called Kamur had decided to relocate to a long, straight stretch of the Kronkel known by the Dutch as "the freeway." Most of the river twisted through the swamp, but here it stretched out for more than a mile.

As the riverboats turned onto "the freeway," the officials blinked at the impressive treehouses of Haenam and then, a few minutes later, Kamur. Smoke still drifted up out of the roofs but there was no one in sight.

"No people," one officer commented. "They've probably run off into the jungle. They may return tomorrow and show themselves. Let's keep going."

Most villagers had fled into the jungle, but some brave men had stayed close by to watch through the trees.

***

The villagers of Haenam and Kamur watched the great river monsters pass, sure their homes were going to be destroyed. They could do nothing to protect themselves. How could bamboo arrows fight swift-moving creatures so large they made the great Kronkel River seem too small to hold them?

As the great beasts passed by, the Sawi stared in disbelief at what they saw. Men, dark-skinned like themselves, rode inside! They spotted others inside the beasts as well—men with faces that shone like fresh, pink sago loaves.

"Tuans!" one Sawi exclaimed, "The Tuans are coming!"

The occupants of the boats waved toward the shore, correctly guessing that human eyes watched.

After the boats left the area, the elders of both Haenam and Kamur talked long into the night trying to figure out what to do when the boats came back downstream. At Kamur, three brave warriors—Nair[3], Kigo, and Numu—volunteered to try to make friendly contact with them.

"Years ago we lived with the Auyu people," they said. "Perhaps some of the strangers speak Auyu and we will be able to talk with them."

Sure enough, the next morning they heard the growing sound of the beasts returning in their direction. Hundreds of eyes watched from the jungle as Nair, Kigo, and Numu stood trembling on the riverbank, holding gifts of food in their quivering hands. Desperately they tried to control the shaking of their knees as the roaring sounds approached.

The first boat swept past them, unnoticing. The three Kamur warriors almost collapsed in relief! Then, as they continued to shakily wave, the second boat stopped its engine and swung toward them. Kigo jabbered nervously in the Auyu language while Nair and Numu nodded their heads.

---

3. Nair's name was really Hato. It has been changed here to avoid confusion with other characters.

A friendly voice called out to them from inside the boat. The greeting party began to relax slightly. Perhaps they would survive this horrible meeting! Welcoming hands reached out from the boats for the gifts of food. Soon they passed back gifts in return. A large, white-faced man spoke with unbelievably strange sounds in a deep, booming voice.

A Tuan!

Minutes later the boats resumed their trip down the river. The three Sawi representatives, faint from nervous strain, turned to see Kamur villagers running from the security of the jungle to congratulate their new heroes!

Nair, Kigo, and Numu proudly held up their treasures—razor blades, matches, fishline, and fishhooks. They had absolutely no idea what the items were or how to use them, but they were proof the men had survived a meeting with Tuans.

Several days later a well-informed Kayagar came down the river and grandly showed the "poor, dumb Sawi" how to remove the razor from its red wrapper. He taught them how to slide the matchbox open, take out a match, and strike it on the side to make fire. "You must put bait on the hook in order to catch a fish," he instructed slowly, as if to ignorant babies. He returned home, laughing at the simplicity of the Sawi, forgetting that only a few months before he himself had learned the same lessons.

CHAPTER 5

THE LEGENDMAKER

The excitement from the riverboat encounter filled the Sawis' minds for several weeks. Even Kani became completely distracted and forgot about his plans of treachery. But only for a short while.

One day, Kani found himself alone when his two wives went off searching the mud banks for shrimp. He took advantage of the solitude to invite Maum, Mavu, and Sauni to his home. Once they settled, he began revealing his plan.

"The Tuans are coming, and we haven't yet gotten revenge for my brother's and our friends' deaths at the hands of Mauro. How do you feel about that?" Kani asked.

The others were ashamed. They knew they should have acted before now, regardless of riverboats and Tuans.

Kani spun his web further. "Maybe you have forgotten, but I cannot forget. We must get revenge before the Tuans come!"

The other men eagerly scanned Kani's face, searching for a clue to his plan.

"Should we sneak into Mauro land and try to kill more of them?"

"No," Kani dropped his voice to build the suspense. "I have a better plan."

"Tell us," Sauni prompted.

"We won't get revenge on Mauro itself. Instead, we will trap the men of Wasohwi, who are related to Mauro. They have some friends here in Haenam. Does that give you an idea?" Kani questioned.

Mavu frowned. "How can we get Wasohwi warriors to come? Won't they know it is a trap?"

"We will announce an all-night dance and send them an invitation," Kani replied.

"Who will take them the invitation? They're not used to any of us, and their friends here won't cooperate with such a plan!"

Kani nodded in agreement and stated firmly, "Our brothers here in the village must know nothing of this plan! They must think this is an honest, sincere invitation. They won't know until they see the dead bodies of their friends!"

"Then who will go and bring the victims back here to us?" Mavu wondered aloud.

Slowly Kani responded, "Remember that one of our own group is related to Wasohwi through his mother. He goes there freely to visit."

The listeners whistled in astonishment. "Paha!" Maum exclaimed. "But how could you possibly *convince* him to betray his own mother's people?"

Kani replied with the answer he had carefully prepared. "We can't convince him to do such a terrible thing," he stated, before adding in a mysterious whisper, "but we can *force* him to do it."

Kani paused as the others leaned forward intently. "We will put the *waness* bind on him. Then he will have to do whatever we say!"

The listeners' eyes rounded with awe at these words. No one had ever dreamed of doing such a thing before! To use the *waness* bind to force a close relative to betray his own mother's people? Unheard of! Filled with devilish treachery. *Legendary.*

Kani had just carried the Sawi dream of treachery to a new level, beyond what his ancestors had achieved. That meant that Kani was a legendmaker, and he offered Maum, Mavu, and Sauni a chance to join him in making this new legend. They, too, would share in the glory and be sung about over fires. They could not pass up this opportunity!

The uniqueness of the idea meant that it might work. Time had passed, and Wasohwi villagers had probably forgotten that Mauro had killed and eaten Kani's Haenam relatives. They would come to the dance expecting Paha to protect them. Nothing in their legends warned that a man might betray his own mother's relatives!

The necessary ingredient to the plan was the use of the *waness* bind to make Paha cooperate. A *waness* bind required a Sawi to do something extremely shameful, forcing someone else to redeem them from that shame by fulfilling a promise that could not be broken.

"Tell us, Kani," Maum asked curiously, "which of us should put the *waness* bind on Paha?"

Kani smiled. He had pulled his friends into his web of treachery easily. They would help him become a master of treachery. Kani had their complete attention and whispered softly, "It will not be one of us."

He paused, letting their curiosity deepen. "No, it will not be one of us. It will have to be your mother, Maum and Sauni. Old Wario will put the *waness* bind on Paha!"

Mavu sat thunderstruck. Maum touched his fingertips to his chest, whistling his amazement. Poor Paha! He was in for a tremendous shock!

The men looked at each other as Kani's genius sank in. Wario, mother of a beautiful young girl whom Paha would soon marry, was the perfect one to put the *waness* bind on Paha. The poor fellow would be trapped by the most sacred relationship imaginable to the Sawi people.

Nothing was more important to a male Sawi than his relationship to his parents-in-law. His respect for them was so deep that he never spoke their names out loud, referring to them only by their titles. He lavished gifts of wild pork or beetle grubs on his in-laws, often before feeding his own family.

Fighting was a way of life for the Sawi people. If trust and peace between men and their in-laws broke down, the Sawi might die out as a people. Now Kani proposed that this most sacred relationship—the one bastion of safety in Sawi society—should be used to force a man to betray his own mother's relatives to death! If old Wario put a *waness* bind on Paha, he would have to do whatever she asked of him, including betraying Wasohwi.

Mavu, Maum, and Sauni could not disguise their awe. They sat with a new hero. He would be a legendmaker, and they could share in the glory! Maum and Sauni immediately gave Kani permission to ask their mother to join in the plan.

✳✳✳

Among the tribes of southwest New Guinea women didn't stand on the sidelines when it came to cruelty. They beat anyone returning from a headhunting raid who failed to bring back a human head and loudly complained about deaths that had not been avenged.

The women adored warriors who returned from a successful raid, encouraging them to risk their lives in pursuit of murder and revenge. Sawi fighters sometimes dragged wounded victims back to their villages so the women might have the pleasure of clubbing them to death.

When a woman played a large role in the betrayal and treachery of *tuwi asonai man,* she was sure to be remembered and become famous. Old Wario knew that as well as any Sawi. Kani was sure she would not keep herself out of the story.

***

Old Wario, head shaved in the custom of Sawi widows, sat nervously thinking about the suggestion of the four men, two of whom were her own sons! They waited as she considered. Her daughter, soon to be married, played outside near the river.

Wario turned to the cooking fire and flipped over some sago loaves. "I have always felt sorry over the deaths of our men," she commented.

Then she added, "Call Paha."

***

Paha climbed into Maum's longhouse and seated himself on a grass mat. Maum, Sauni, Mavu, and Kani kept up a casual conversation to draw his attention away from Wario. She fiddled with the fire before picking up one of the sago loaves she had just finished cooking. Wario pretended to offer Paha a sago loaf and he reached to take it. But she ignored his hand and touched him with the loaf. Then she leapt back and took a bite of the same loaf. This was a disgraceful act and put him in her debt. The only way he could remove the debt was to offer to do whatever she asked. Horror flooded into his eyes as he realized what she had done. He cringed, trapped.

Waness!

Paha realized with horror that his future was about to take a drastic turn. He could not escape whatever command his mother-in-law would now give him, no matter the personal cost. Otherwise, his entire community at Haenam would turn against him. Obviously, the task Wario had for him would be something terrible—why else would she have used the *waness* bind?

Paha stared at the grass mat. Finally, after several minutes of silent torment, he croaked out, "What do you want me to do?"

***

The news spread like fire. All the Sawi heard, as did the Atohwaem, Auyu, Kayagar, and Asmat tribes. The news overwhelmed the jungle like the Kronkel flooding its banks. Paha had betrayed his own mother's people! Haenam village became famous, admired, and feared.

In Wasohwi village, mourners rolled in ashes, voices hoarse from wailing, eyes reddened with burning tears. Eight men from Wasohwi had trustingly accepted Paha's invitation to the all-night dance in Haenam. They arrived just as the men of Haenam began to beat on their drums. Kani, one of the most important villagers, welcomed the guests.

Dancers gathered under treehouses, shouting and chanting at the stars. Occasionally the drumbeat picked up. One of the dancers would raise his voice and boast of a murder he had committed and everyone else fell silent to listen. Then they would all begin shouting again. Several minutes later another warrior proclaimed his role in a killing. The booming of the drums between speakers symbolized the long intervals of plotting and waiting before each recounted act of treachery.

The Wasohwi visitors danced and ate heartily with their hosts, never dreaming that Paha had betrayed them to be the dessert for the feast.

Shortly before dawn Kani invited his chosen victim, Fusuman, into his treehouse to smoke. Sauni, Mavu, Maum, and four others also took "guests" to their homes. Not a hint of the danger showed. Some of the Haenam villagers themselves knew absolutely nothing of the horror coiling around the eight visitors.

***

Once Fusuman was seated comfortably and smoking a bamboo pipe, Kani came up behind him with a steel machete he had received in trade from a Kayagar. He struck a hard blow to the base of Fusuman's skull.

Fusuman jerked forward, gagging. The machete blade was very dull. Fusuman rolled over and stared up in horror as Kani raised his other new possession, a steel axe.

"No, Kani, brother!" he gasped.

"Don't call me 'brother,'" Kani sneered, "for I am killing you!"

Kani struck Fusuman again and again with his axe. The sounds woke his wives, who fanned the fire to life in time to see Kani behead Fusuman.

Kani then ran to Maum's treehouse and climbed the ladder. "Have you killed yours yet?" he whispered.

Maum stretched lazily and replied, "Not yet."

"What are you waiting for?" Kani taunted. "I have already beheaded mine!"

Maum whistled his admiration and turned back into his house. Kani hurried down the ladder. He heard the thud of a spear and a strangled cry. He did not notice the wounded victim scrambling down the ladder behind him. By the time Maum found a second spear, his victim had vanished in the darkness, leaving only a trail of blood.

Mavu also tried to kill his guest, but only wounded him. His victim screamed out a warning to his friends as he fled. The thunder of the drums drowned out his cries.

Three other visitors were killed and beheaded. The four Wasohwi survivors struggled home through miles of swamp and jungle, only to die from their wounds as they reached the ladders of their longhouses.

***

Weeks of celebration at Haenam followed the murders. The villagers openly adored Kani and Paha. The fact that four of the eight victims escaped beheading and cannibalization did not take away from the honor. The number of heads didn't matter, only the quality of the betrayal.

Kani and Paha had taken the ideal of using friendship to fatten one's victim for the slaughter to a new level. The Sawi found comfort and delight in the misery and destruction of others. Kani's cleverness and treachery made him an ideal Sawi man.

The legendmaker's place of respect, however, was soon to be challenged. Not only his place, but the whole Sawi idea of honoring treachery. A contest of values was coming, riding in on the waves of the Kronkel.

Kani and Paha had no idea that long ago a completely different kind of Legendmaker had demonstrated a radical new ideal based on love. It had taken nearly two thousand years for the message of this new value system to spread from Galilee, in the Middle East, to the humid swamps of southwest New Guinea.

The message had already challenged and conquered all kinds of evil. Nothing could intimidate it, for it was the perfect cure for fear. No darkness could hide it, for it was light itself! Much to the frustration of its enemies, this message won even when those who followed it were killed by sword or spear.

The message was the good news of Jesus Christ. Its goal: to bring people from "every tribe, and tongue, and people, and nation" into a right relationship with God through Jesus Christ. The gospel of love was about to invade the Sawi world and confront their long-held ideas. It would pit prayer and preaching against spear and arrow, love and compassion against fear and evil, faith against cruelty, forgiveness against betrayal.

The first of the true Legendmaker's message-carriers were preparing to come and live with the Sawi on the banks of the Twisted River.

CHAPTER 6

SUMMONS TO THE UNKNOWN

A slender, seventy-one-year-old Englishman gripped the edge of a lectern with his bony hands. He studied the seven hundred students who waited in silence to hear him speak. Finally he rumbled three words:

"Netherlands New Guinea..."

Dr. Ebenezer Vine, representing the mission society Regions Beyond Missionary Union (RBMU), introduced his topic with those words in 1955. Students at the Prairie Bible Institute of Alberta, Canada, leaned forward in their chairs, hanging on every word.

"Netherlands New Guinea," Dr. Vine repeated, "is the western half of a 1,400-mile-long island stretched along the edge of the Pacific Ocean north of Australia. It lies in the tropics, just south of the equator. Yet, within its 110,000 square miles, you will find jagged mountain ranges with ice at their 15,000-foot peaks. You will also find steamy swamps where pounding rains join with unbearable heat, creating sweltering humidity.

"Will you be the first to go to an entire tribe that has never known any kind of governmental control? A group who have their own laws and where violence and brutality are a way of life? You will need to make yourself and your message understood in languages never before learned by an outsider. You will find no help in dictionaries or books. You will have to make those yourself.

"You will find customs and beliefs which will completely baffle you, but you must understand them if you are to succeed. You will find horrible tropical diseases to treat and perhaps be blamed for the death of the patient if you fail. You will have to endure loneliness, frustration, and exhaustion with patience and strength. You must be prepared in the strength of the Lord to do battle with the prince of darkness, who, having held these tribes captive for thousands of years, is not about to give them up without a fight."

Dr. Vine paused, letting his words sink in.

"We have asked the Netherlands government for permission to enter this land and were at first denied. The government would not accept the responsibility of protecting missionaries from cannibals! We kept asking for permission—and recently we received it.

"The way is now open to the hidden parts of the island! We already have four workers in New Guinea, living with tribes. The island is open for more. I cannot believe that God has given this opportunity for only four workers! There must be others He wants to go. Has He prepared you for this task?

"How much longer must these lost tribes wait to hear of Him who died for their salvation and rose again to give them eternal life? Our Lord wants to establish His kingdom of love in those dark, fearful places! He wants to drive out cruelty and pain. Four people have gone ahead to begin the work. Who will go and help them?"

Throughout the auditorium those words stirred the hearts of many young men and women. Dozens of Prairie students set their sights on going to Netherlands New Guinea to share the love of Christ. Some would end up giving their lives to see the church begin.

Twenty-year-old Don Richardson was one of the students sitting in the auditorium. As he listened, he felt God's hand on him. He returned to his dorm room to pray. *Is this it, Lord? Is this what You want me to do?* he asked.

Don had accepted Jesus as his Lord and Savior just three years earlier, at the age of seventeen. He knew that in any crisis, Jesus was there, alive! Two thousand years had not aged Jesus at all. He still had power to change people's lives. Don desired to know Him and share Him with others. If sharing Jesus where His name was already known was a privilege, taking news of Him to a place His name had never been heard must be an even greater privilege! Don heard an inner voice confirm, *This is it! I want you to go!*

Another Prairie student, Carol Soderstrom, also felt God calling her to work in Netherlands New Guinea. Don and Carol were classmates and became good friends. Sensing that God was calling them to each other as well as to the tribes, they eventually married. Carol went on to train as a nurse while Don served as a pastor and youth worker. Their preparation would prove to be very important in the journey ahead.

In March of 1962 Don and Carol Richardson boarded a boat bound for the South Pacific with their four-month-old son, Stephen. A month later they stepped off a small plane in the highland interior of New Guinea and were welcomed by former Prairie classmates.

The next day, Don went for a walk with one of the missionaries. "We have some workers, John and Glenna McCain, who have recently started to work among a group called the Kayagar, down in the southern swamps," he mentioned to Don. "They tell us the area is anything but pleasant. Many of the tribes still practice cannibalism and headhunting. They're not to be trusted. The climate is as hot, humid, and unhealthy as it could possibly be.

"Despite the risks, we agreed to ask you and Carol to consider going there. We realize that you might not want to, especially because of your little boy. If you'd rather work somewhere else, just say so. But if God gives you peace about going to one of the tribes in that area, the way is open to you."

Don and Carol spent the next two days praying, studying their Bibles, and listening. Then they gave their answer. "We'd be happy to go to one of the tribes in the south! How soon can we leave?"

The Richardsons flew to the southern lowlands on May 19. The mighty mountains of the interior suddenly dropped from more than 15,000 feet to sea level. Shimmering, emerald-green swamps crisscrossed by brown rivers stretched as far as the eye could see. Somewhere in the midst of that patchwork, Don and Carol would build a home and live with cannibal-headhunters.

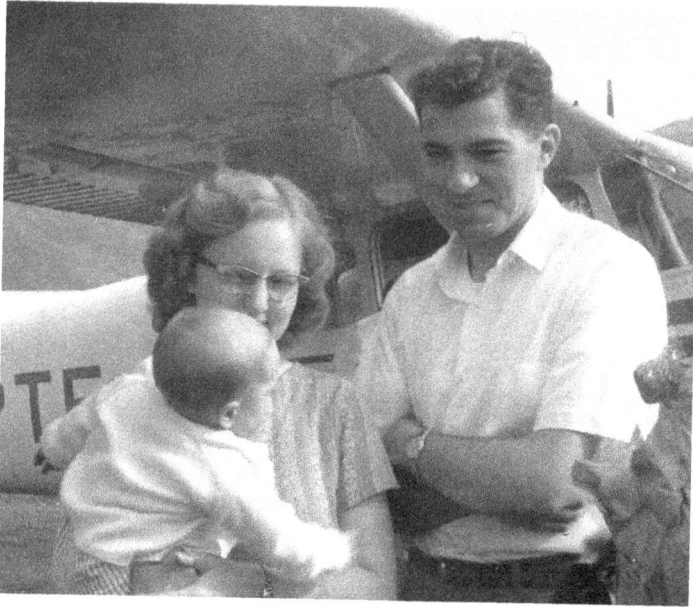

Carol and Don Richardson, with their six-month-old son, Stephen

The small plane landed at a Dutch outpost called Pirimapun, located on the Arafura Sea.

The following morning the Richardsons traveled forty miles by boat up the Cook River. John and Glenna McCain lived and ministered in a Kayagar village deep in the sago swamps. The McCains suggested that Don and Carol begin work among a tribe living to the northwest of the Kayagar—the Sawi.

Sawi! After years of preparing and waiting, just hearing the name excited Don and Carol. They could hardly wait to go!

CHAPTER 7

THROUGH THE IRONWOOD CURTAIN

The *Ebenezer* rocked gently at the dock as John and Don loaded fuel and supplies onto the river launch. Kayagar longhouses, like black logs placed in two long rows, were visible in the distance. Inside the McCains' house, Glenna and Carol packed meals for their husbands by the light of kerosene lamps.

At 5:30 a.m. the boat's Volkswagen engine roared to life. John pointed the bow downstream. Glenna and Carol, holding Stephen, waved goodbye.

John and Don traveled down the Cook River to Pirimapun and along the edge of the Arafura Sea. Then they reached the mouth of the Kronkel River and entered Sawi territory. They passed dense sago thickets, swarms of white egrets, hordes of giant fruit bats, and camouflaged crocodiles and pythons, not knowing they were following the same twisting course the Dutch riverboats had taken two years before.

In the first three Sawi villages they encountered, the women and children fled into the jungle at the boat's approach, but some men stayed on shore to meet the Tuans. Don learned a few Sawi words during these brief encounters—a small start on a language made up of several thousand terms.

A fourth village, Sato, stood empty, the inhabitants having fled in terror. Don climbed up into one of the treehouses and left a small gift in the center of the floor to show his goodwill. Then he and John pressed on, hoping to find a large population of Sawi on the Kronkel. They found none that day, so they anchored in the middle of the river for another night.

The following morning the men decided to leave the slower *Ebenezer* at anchor and head off in a smaller skiff that they had been towing. They passed the mouth of the Hanai tributary, unaware that it led to the hideaway where Kani and his co-conspirators had killed and eaten four Wasohwi guests.

Swinging around a sharp bend, they found the decaying remnants of the Kamur village where Nair, Kigo, and Numu had met their first Tuans. The village had been located on "the freeway" then, but the tribe had moved on, as was their custom, and the structures were now so overgrown with vines that Don hardly noticed them.

"This straight stretch of river just might make an excellent landing site for a float plane," Don remarked. "That would help with getting supplies."

The men steered the boat toward the muddy bank and stepped ashore at the same spot where Nair, Kigo, and Numu had stood two years earlier when they faced the Dutch riverboats.

Sawi men with ornately carved shields

No welcome committee waited this time. The jungle felt like a brooding, dark presence taunting Don. *You are not equal to me. I am not at all like your tame Canadian homeland. I am tangled, hot, and drenched with rain. I am hip-deep mud and six-inch sago thorns. I am death adder snakes and taipans, leeches and crocodiles. I am terrible diseases like malaria, dysentery, and hepatitis.*

Your good intentions mean nothing here. Your Christian gospel will never reach the hearts of my jungle people. You only think you love them, but wait until you really know them—if you ever can know them! You think you're ready to wrestle with me, understand my mysteries, change my nature. But I will be able to overpower you easily with my gloom, my brutality, my complete otherness!

Think again, before you commit yourself to certain failure! Can't you see that I am no place for your wife? I am no place for your son! I am no place for you…

John waited by the skiff.

It's only the enemy trying to discourage me, Don thought. *This swamp is also part of the Father's creation. He can keep me here just as well as He can keep me anywhere.* God's peace surrounded Don. "I want to build my house here!" he announced to John, who nodded in agreement.

***

Kani and thirty-nine other warriors cautiously pushed their dugouts through the winding Hanai tributary. Packs of fresh sago flour and toasted beetle grubs filled the spaces between the feet of the paddlers. Lori parrots fluttered on the ends of tethers like red, blue, and green balloons. Chickens poked their heads over the sago packs.

The forty adventurers from Haenam had decided to journey to Pirimapun, the nearest government outpost. For two years they had heard fantastic stories about the riches of that place. Many times they had unsuccessfully tried to gather enough courage to make the frightful journey. Now they determined to go!

The day before, they had hidden their women, children, and possessions deep in the jungle. Just after sunrise they reached the mouth of the Hanai tributary.

Kani crouched down to peer through the branches screening the murky Kronkel River. It would be a fatal mistake to burst into the open water and find oneself face to face with Asmat warriors! The Kronkel was empty, so Kani paddled powerfully out into the open. The others followed.

With the tips of their spear-paddles scissoring over their heads they turned upstream to take the long way to Pirimapun. They planned to reach the Cook River to the south by cutting through flooded Kayagar grasslands in order to avoid the hostile Asmat villages that menaced the more direct route by the Kronkel. The Kayagar tribe was becoming increasingly friendly toward the Sawi, but just in case, the Haenam canoes were lined with forty palmwood bows and hundreds of barb-tipped arrows.

The Sawi adventurers had already committed themselves to the long "freeway" of the Kronkel when their courage was tested to its limit. Straight ahead, just out of sight around the bend of the "freeway," a sound like the whine of an angry wasp split the quiet of the morning. It grew louder, heading straight toward them!

A pale yellow boat suddenly burst into sight, streamers of spray shooting out behind it. In the craft were two figures wearing bright-colored skins. *Tuans!*

Pandemonium exploded in the four Haenam canoes. The appearance of the skiff threw the Sawi into complete confusion. Some of the men leaped from their canoes and plunged among the reeds. Others waved their paddles frantically, trying to stay balanced.

There was no time to escape. Within seconds the skiff pulled up beside the Sawi. John called out to them in Kayagar, encouraging them to have no fear. Among the Haenam men was the Atohwaem warrior Hadi, who spoke both Kayagar and Sawi. He quickly translated John's reassurances into Sawi.

The slender, hard-muscled warriors stood trembling, causing their dugouts to shiver. Don reached out, touching fingertips with the nearest men, and called the Sawi greeting, *"Konahario!"* Hearing it, the men released their nervous tension by shouting back, *"Konahario!"*

One by one, the Haenam men who had hidden themselves among the reeds swam out and climbed back into their canoes. John and Don passed out a dozen empty tin cans which they had saved for such an occasion. Tin cans were highly prized by the Sawi, whose only water containers were lengths of hollow bamboo. The cans would be used and reused until they rusted away.

Hadi told John that the men were on an expedition to Pirimapun.

"This is a big adventure for them!" John exclaimed to Don. "It's probably the first time in their history that they have gone outside their own land to meet with civilization. And God timed our trip so we would meet them within the first few miles of their journey!" John was right, for if they had started a few minutes earlier, they would have passed the mouth of the Hanai before the Haenam expedition emerged.

John invited Hadi to make the journey back to Pirimapun with them in the skiff so Don could learn more of the Sawi language.

Hadi, upon hearing the invitation, turned pale in spite of his dark skin! To accept the offer meant committing his life to the uncertain ways of these bizarre and possibly non-human beings. He would also have to travel with them into the fearful Asmat region. Then he would have to travel on the ocean—an experience completely beyond his imagination.

Although Hadi had lived all his life only twenty air miles from the Arafura Sea, he had never once seen it. He had, however, heard several awe-inspiring reports of what the sea was like. During the monsoon storms he had heard the distant thunder of its mighty waves pounding night and day. How terrible to be close to the source of that impressive sound!

On the other hand, what an adventure Hadi would have! And how impressed all his friends would be *if* he returned safely. He could tell the story to at least three tribes, as he spoke that many languages. He would learn much about the Tuans, preparing the way for future contacts with them.

The hoped-for benefits, Hadi decided, outweighed the potential dangers. "I'll go with you," he finally told John. Hadi's Sawi friends stared at him, concerned about his safety.

John wisely invited a second person to accompany Hadi to help him feel more comfortable on the journey. A smiling youth named Er courageously accepted the offer. After both settled in the skiff, Ken restarted the motor and headed off on the forty winding river-miles to the Arafura Sea.

***

Thirty minutes later, the men found the *Ebenezer* still anchored in the Kronkel. They climbed aboard and continued toward the sea. Don, Hadi, and Er began language lessons.

When the men neared the Asmat villages, Hadi and Er became very nervous. Their tension ebbed away as the Asmat simply lined up along the shore to stare at the *Ebenezer* as it left its wake at their feet.

As they rounded the last bend of the Kronkel and faced the open sea, Hadi and Er gasped. The late afternoon sun made the water gleam so brightly it hurt their eyes to look at it. Hadi and Er must have thought they were traveling into nothingness itself as they headed out into the shiny expanse.

The boat began to rock with the ocean swells. Hadi and Er clasped the handrails, fearing the launch might capsize. Don laid his hand on Hadi's shoulder, whispering two Sawi words Hadi himself had just taught him, "*Tadan nom!* Don't be afraid!"

Hadi looked at Don, smiling cautiously. "I am not afraid!" he claimed, then released the handrail to prove it.

***

At one o'clock in the morning Don and John finally saw the McCains' house. Their first journey to the Sawi was over. Don stepped onto the dock as Carol raced down to hug him.

"Is everything all right?" Don asked.

"Just perfect!" she replied.

"Guess what? We have two Sawi speakers on board!" Don grinned. Carol peered curiously past Don's shoulder at Hadi and Er. She smiled.

After setting up a place for Hadi and Er to stay, Don and Carol crept into the room where Stephen slept. Whatever future awaited them with the Sawi, their six-month-old son would share it.

Don and Carol felt a spirit of trust giving them confidence. They would build a house and live at the site of the abandoned village that Don had learned was called Kamur. God would protect them and their family from any danger. They took comfort in the verse, "If God is for us, who can be against us?" (Romans 8:31).

The Richardsons' peace and excitement seemed to come from God Himself, who had been waiting such a long, long time to work His wonders among the Sawi. He was delighted that at last the time had come! Don had never realized before that God could feel *excited.*

Don and Carol pleaded with God to break through all cultural or spiritual barriers so that His message of redemption in Christ could reach the Sawi. The Sawi needed joy to replace their fear!

***

The following day a shout went up from the Kayagar village. The Sawi had arrived! Hadi and Er waved eagerly, and all four dugouts veered straight to the McCains' dock.

The thirty-eight paddlers felt nervous and out of place as they beached their canoes. Far from his own home, Kani felt the strangeness of their expedition. And they still had another forty miles to paddle before reaching Pirimapun!

Hadi and Er decided to remain with Don to work on language, so the Haenam expedition continued on without them. Two days later they returned, having sold their goods in the "big city" of Pirimapun. Hadi and Er joined them for the return trip home.

"You should spend some time fishing on the Kronkel for a few days," John stated.

Hadi smiled as he translated the message into Sawi. It meant they should keep lookouts posted because the Tuans intended to return some day soon.

Don had easily won the friendship of Hadi and Er—but what about the other grim, determined warriors? It was too early to tell what reaction the majority of the Sawi would have, but soon he would find out.

CHAPTER 8

THE END OF AN AGE

One Kayagar dugout wobbled under the weight of two empty 55-gallon steel drums. The other canoe comfortably held a large mosquito net, bedroll, a week's supply of food, tools for building, and trade goods to pay workers.

Just after 7 a.m. on that June day, 1962, Don kissed Carol and Stephen goodbye and climbed into the goods-laden canoe. He took along a container of boiled drinking water. Don planned to take the shortcut by dugout through the Kayagar swamps to the abandoned Kamur village. Once there he would renew contact with the Sawi and start building a house.

The jungle stillness draped itself over Don and the six Kayagar paddlers. The paddles swishing in the still water and reeds rubbing against the dugouts made the only sounds. Sometimes the sun peeked out through the gray sky, making the sago forests glow.

Once the paddlers reached the sago thickets, the waterway narrowed. For two hours they followed a twisting channel, then broke out onto the grasslands that drain into the Kronkel River. Three other Kayagar canoes appeared, and their occupants reached out to grip Don's arms. They shouted and pointed ahead.

The Kayagar realized from the building materials filling his canoes that Don planned to build a home somewhere in the area. They wanted him to build his house at their village, Amyam.

Don couldn't understand all the words, but they seemed to say something like, "Tuan, don't go to the Sawi! They kill and eat people! Come to our village! We have plenty of high ground for houses. Come to our village! Come to our village! Come!"

Don vainly tried to dampen their hopes, but he didn't have enough words in the Kayagar language. He tried to get his paddlers to explain to the strangers that Don wanted to go to the Sawi village called Kamur. His Kayagar paddlers had no interest in sharing that piece of news.

The Kayagar did not want to see the Sawi get steel axes, machetes, and other trade goods, which they knew would eventually follow wherever the Tuans went. Don realized that his paddlers and the strangers were working together to pressure him into changing his mind.

John McCain had warned Don that before long the people in the area would test his will to see if they could intimidate him into doing what they wanted. "You must pass that test!" John's voice echoed in Don's mind.

The Kayagar shouted and argued with Don for two hours. Other canoes joined the floating group as it moved through the grasslands, raising the volume and putting more pressure on him. Don realized he could not reason with them in any language so he sat quietly, waiting.

Unfortunately, the Kayagar took his silence as acceptance. They started to whoop and holler—they were going to have their very own Tuan!

Don looked up to see the Amyam village straight ahead. The Kayagar began to thump their paddle blades on the sides of their canoes, announcing their triumphant arrival with a Tuan.

Don spoke forcefully in mixed Kayagar and Indonesian, "*Sevi terus ke Kamur!* Go straight on to Kamur!"

His paddlers reluctantly turned his canoe toward Kamur, but a large, swift Kayagar dugout lurched forward, curved in front of Don's canoe, and forced it over to the shore. Kayagar villagers rushed out, calling to Don, waving, and pleading.

Don hated to disappoint them, but knew he must be firm. He rose to his feet in the canoe, looking down from his six-foot-two-inch frame at the Kayagar crowded around him. "*Go straight to Kamur!*" he roared.

Silence. For a few seconds Don was uncertain whether the men would accept or resent his demand. Slowly, sulkily, the men in the large dugout moved aside. Don and his paddlers continued on their way.

Don had passed the first test, but he felt very sad. As a messenger of Christ, it was hard to refuse this hearty invitation from such a needy people. However, Don knew that John McCain would soon be able to share the Good News with the Kayagar in their own language. That fact made their need somewhat less urgent than that of the Sawi, who still had no messenger of Christ who could speak their language.

***

The steady Kronkel current carried Don's canoes past an area that served as a "no-man's-land" during troubled times. The Kayagar paddlers pointed out various tributaries that emptied into the Kronkel and named the villages found on each of the tributaries.

"That water leads to Yohwi, where Hadi lives," one paddler commented.

"Hadi!" Don exclaimed. "Quick! Turn in and take me to Hadi! I want to see him before we go to Kamur."

The men paddled for about a mile into the thick jungle. Off in the distance Don could see a clearing with six longhouses.

"Hadi," the paddlers called, "Tuan Don is here!"

Some of the napping villagers scrambled to their feet, prepared to flee. Others took the time to see who was outside. Hadi was out in the jungle working, but messengers soon found him and brought him back.

"Come into my home, Tuan," Hadi greeted Don. They climbed up together, then the two sat down to chat, using all of Don's few Sawi words. Although Don had no idea how to put the words together properly, Hadi seemed to understand what he was trying to say.

Don mentioned that he wanted to build a home at Kamur. Hadi sat stunned, wondering if he had misunderstood Don's chopped-up Sawi. Don repeated the message. Turning to those gathered around, Hadi translated the news into Atohwaem for them. Whistles and excited exclamations greeted the announcement.

"I want you to come to Kamur and help me build my home, Hadi," Don shared.

"Good," Hadi replied, a wide smile breaking out on his face. "I'll come tomorrow."

After hugging Hadi goodbye, Don continued on his journey.

***

By five o'clock that afternoon Don and the Kayagar paddlers reached the old, rotting village of Kamur. There was no sign of any Sawi in the area. Don didn't have time to go look for any, either, as only one hour of daylight remained. He and his Kayagar helpers chose the least run-down-looking of the dilapidated long-houses and hauled their goods up into it. The poles supported their weight, but they had to be careful not to step through one of the huge holes in the floor!

Shortly before dawn they awoke to the roar of an approaching wall of rain. Within seconds it struck the old longhouse with so much force that the building shivered and swayed on its rotting poles. The storm dumped rain until mid-morning.

Once the skies cleared, Don sent two of the Kayagar paddlers up a tributary to find the villagers of Kamur at their new location. They carried gifts for the chiefs and planned to invite them to come meet the Tuan. Three others set out with axes to cut ironwood logs for the foundation of Don's home. The remaining Kayagar paddler, Hedip, stayed behind to help Don clear the land.

The tangled mass of vines covering the ground fought back against their machetes, but Don and Hedip kept hacking. All the ground they cleared was low, about the same level as the river. Don wanted to build on higher land, otherwise water would stand under the floor of the house for months at a time. Don and Hedip continued slashing.

Hedip pointed his machete toward the twisted roots at his feet. The land sloped upward! It rose to an unbelievable height of four feet above the surrounding swampland. Land that high would be dry most of the year. Stephen would have a dry place to play after all!

Two hours later the two gift-bearers returned, grinning happily. "We found them, Tuan," they reported.

"Where are they?" Don asked.

The Kayagar pointed upstream. Don saw five dugouts inching closer, almost blocked from sight by a screen of plants. The Kayagar called to them, and finally one canoe peeked out, followed by another. The Sawi warriors stared silently at Don. They slowly crept forward, encouraged by the Kayagar.

"Konahario!" Don called.

No reply. The Sawi stared. They trembled a bit as they silently watched Don. Don trembled too, but on the inside. There was no John to give advice and no *Ebenezer* to hop into if the meeting went badly.

Don and the Sawi appeared completely alien to each other. Meeting a stranger is difficult enough, but meeting one who was so different seemed impossible!

Three of the older Sawi stepped ashore and approached Don. The Kayagar, having failed in their quest to keep Don to themselves, now took pride in their role as mediators between Don and the Sawi. They coaxed and cajoled until the Sawi came closer.

One of the three Kamur leaders suddenly stepped right up to Don. His right eye had been pierced with an arrow and had rotted out. His left eye gleamed. Don and the tribesman extended their hands and as they touched fingers, the feeling of strangeness fled. They were equals... flesh and blood... human.

The Sawi man smiled at Don and announced, "I am Nair!"

Don gripped his hand and replied, "I am Don!"

The two other Sawi crowded in, touching Don's hand.

"I am Kigo!" announced one.

"I am Numu!"

The three heroes had come out to meet a Tuan again!

Their friends rushed up from the canoes, shouting *Konaharios!* Don pointed to the recently cleared land and used sign language to show he meant to build a house. He asked the Kamur villagers to bring palm tree bark for the floor. They promised to return with it the next day.

Cries of rejoicing split the air. All the men shouted together, since no one expressed his joy fully unless they all expressed it together.

Then still more shouting broke out from behind Don. He swung around to find the Kronkel black with canoes. Hadi had arrived with a Yohwi crowd rumbling their paddle blades against the sides of their dugouts in celebration. The shouting swelled and broke over and over. It signaled the end of an age of isolation, the beginning of a time of interacting with the outside world.

***

If Don Richardson had not come that day as a messenger of Christ, someone else would have come later—probably with very different motives and results. The world is not big enough for any group of people to remain isolated. Missionaries go to tribal groups to *give*, while lumbermen, crocodile hunters, prospectors, and farmers go in to *take*. Someone will inevitably reach every tribe, no matter how remote. Will the kindest, most sympathetic people get there first?

Don, as the first outsider to live with the Sawi, valued both faithfulness to God and the Scriptures and respect for the Sawi and their culture. He worried, though, whether the Sawi culture and the Scriptures might prove to be so far apart that he would not be able to present God's truth in a way that resonated for the Sawi people.

CHAPTER 9

GODS FROM THE SKY

Word of Don's arrival had spread up the river to nearby Haenam. Kani and other villagers swiftly paddled to join the crowd in Kamur. Don became a lone white speck in the midst of two hundred Kayagar, Atohwaem, and Sawi representing three tribes who had frequently regarded each other as enemies and seldom as friends. Most of the men carried their spear-paddles or had bone daggers stuck in their armbands. Don kept checking over his shoulder, hoping to squelch any conflicts before they could turn violent.

Hours passed, and Don felt God's deep peace settle on him as he worked. He began to speak with more authority, making the few Sawi words he knew go a long way.

A pile-driving operation Don set up captivated the men's attention. Groups climbed onto a platform, raised a heavy piece of log, and let it fall on a post, driving it deep into the soil. The Sawi had never thought of doing things this way. They laughed, and their excitement filled the air.

But once the pile-driving ended, the murmurings and hard looks reappeared between members of different tribes. A tall Kayagar chief let out a rush of words. Don could not tell if he was trying to keep the peace or was expressing some of his own bitterness toward the Sawi. Fearing the latter, Don stepped behind him and gently placed a hand on his shoulder. He knew no Kayagar words to express his feelings, so he simply talked soothingly in English. The chief and others quieted down.

Mutterings of tension between tribes soon began to boil again. Don did not want the day of his arrival to become a day of bloodshed. He laid his tools down and prayed, simply asking God to step in. At that moment the hum of a small plane sounded from the heavens. The angry warriors instantly quieted.

Of course! In the excitement of the afternoon Don had forgotten the scheduled float plane test landing on the Kronkel. The plane carried a load of kerosene to fill Don's steel drums. Don had tried to warn the warriors about the plane's visit, but found he didn't have the words. The warriors had seen or heard airplanes before, passing at great heights. They were convinced that all aircraft were supernatural beings; they had not linked them to Tuans.

When a plane came near, the warriors typically fled into the underbrush of the jungle to hide in terror. One tribesman had suggested that aircraft were allergic to thorns. This was logical, as no airplane does well with thorns in its tires. However, it also caused much pain to the Sawi. They dove into thorns to hide from the planes, then spent days picking the spikes out of their skin!

Don watched as the warriors searched the sky, trying to spot the noisy intruder and hoping it would pass by. Suddenly there it was—low and black in the distance—heading straight toward them! Panic broke out as men and boys stampeded toward the jungle, terrified.

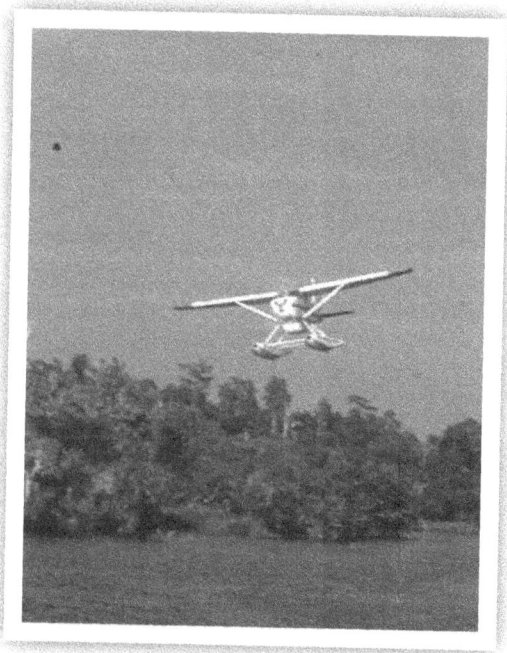

A floatplane lands on the Kronkel near Kamur.

Don waved to the pilot as he zoomed over on the first pass. He then walked down to the riverbank to await the landing. Huddled together, trembling in fear, a small group of tribesmen waited near Don.

Nair and Kigo crouched among the group. Apparently they had understood Don's earlier attempts to explain the airplane and decided it meant them no harm. They wanted to see what would happen when the god from the ground met the god from the sky.

***

The pilots of the mission float plane carefully eyed the long black ribbon of the Kronkel "freeway," searching for anything that could damage the aircraft. Once satisfied that the site was clear, they buzzed the surface, then roared over the treetops. They needed to verify that they would have enough room to take off. Satisfied with the river as a runway, they circled back to land.

***

Nair cowered behind Don, his body streaming with sweat. His one eye followed the downward flight of the Cessna plane. Kigo and the others shuddered and backed away as spray splattered out from under the floats.

When the engine stopped, the shouting of the warriors took over. Dozens of men, arms stretched out, wiggled their fingers toward the plane, trying to keep it away.

The door of the plane opened. Cries of alarm split the air, then faded to gasps of amazement as the pilots climbed down to the floats. Airplanes were vehicles to move the Tuans around!

The plane floats settled into the muddy silt about ten feet from shore. Don waded out to unload some of the kerosene. At first none of the Sawi came close to help, but gradually Don coaxed Nair and Kigo forward. They touched hands with the pilots and saw they were human beings, just like Don.

Before long other warriors waded out under the yellow and black wings to help unload the plane. Don opened one of the empty fifty-five-gallon drums and began funneling kerosene into it. The warriors in the jungle continued shouting and leaping about.

One of the pilots gazed questioningly at Don. "Is everything all right?" he asked.

"Fine," Don replied. He didn't mention that the plane's arrival had probably stopped the outbreak of a fight between three war-like tribes.

Late in the afternoon, as they prepared to leave, the pilot leaned out the door of the plane. He gazed at the wild-eyed, stringy-haired men with curved pig tusks reaching out from their nostrils.

"From the look of things, humanly speaking, I'd say, 'Get in this plane and let us get you out of here!'" he commented. "But I'm guessing you don't want to leave." He was testing Don to see if he'd lost his nerve and needed to be rescued.

"You're right," Don grinned. "I'm just getting started!"

"Okay," the pilot returned. "We'll be praying for you! Take care!"

The door of the plane slammed shut and Don pushed the aircraft around to face the open channel of the Kronkel.

The engine roared to life. Spray pelted Don and the warriors like driving rain. The Cessna raced down the "freeway," lifted above the trees, and vanished in the low-hanging clouds.

***

Some tribesmen decided to return to their villages before the sun set. Don gave them instructions about the sort of jungle building materials he needed the next day if they chose to return to work. Other warriors decided to sleep in the broken-down long-houses so they would be available for work first thing in the morning.

Finally, Don had an opportunity to bathe. Without the commotion of the airplane and crowd to scare away potential predators, Don was too cautious of crocodiles and poisonous snakes to risk a dip in the Kronkel itself. Instead, he stood near the river in his shorts and scooped up buckets of water. He poured the water over himself, soaped up, and rinsed off.

All the remaining tribesmen left their cooking fires to watch the Tuan's strange behavior. They had never seen soap. Don felt their eyes scorching his white skin and wondered about their excited murmurs.

Later he learned that it was not his white skin they were discussing. They were watching the soap suds flow into the Kronkel from Don's skin and wondering what would happen. A foreign substance of potentially great consequence had been introduced to their river—Don's skin grease!

"What will the spirits think?" they asked. "How will they react?"

For better or worse, Don had indeed placed his skin-grease into the Kronkel River. He did not know that in the eyes of the villagers this simple action meant challenging the demons who claimed control of the Sawi and the other tribes.

The challenge had been issued. The response could come at any time.

***

That night Don dreamed he was standing near the giant buttress roots of ironwood trees. He felt dread as he sank to his ankles in the soft jungle mud.

Sawi men came out from the roots, led by one-eyed Nair. Nair's lips moved, but Don heard no voice. Kigo joined Nair, both of them pleading with their eyes. Other faces swam into Don's sight. All looked doomed. All knew they had some deep need they could not satisfy. All urgently begged for release.

Don suddenly awoke, sweating, flooded with a deep desire to bring peace to these grim, lost people. He prayed desperately for an hour, pleading with God to help him share the freedom and peace paid for by Jesus' blood so long ago. Jesus loved these lost sheep of the swamps. Just before sunrise, God breathed in the calmness and assurance Don was seeking. God wanted Sawi in His kingdom. He would help Don share the Good News.

***

Early morning birds greeted dawn with their boisterous calls. Birds-of-paradise, cockatoos, loris, and dozens of other species raised their voices together to welcome the new day. Don and the tribesmen rose and resumed work. They built walls, doors, windows, porch stairs, and a crude kitchen counter. Sawi and Kayagar workers completed a thatched roof and filled in the walls with sago fronds.

On July 10, Don paid the workers and set off to gather his family. "In three days I will return with my wife and child!" he promised.

CHAPTER 10

DESTINY IN A DUGOUT

Snowy egrets flew from tree to tree, appearing to guide the dugout across an ocean of grass. Six Kayagar men propelled a narrow canoe mile after steamy mile through the flooded grassland.

Sitting toward the back of the dugout Don saw Stephen's bright, curious blue eyes peek at him over Carol's shoulder. They widened in delight upon seeing Don and popped with wonder again as the egrets flew by. Stephen laughed, his happy voice mingling with the swish of reeds. Just seven months old, Stephen found his new environment delightful. He sensed none of the danger—only the beauty. At length, lulled by the gentle rocking of the canoe, he fell asleep in the shade of a canopy Don had put up in the center of the dugout.

The sun passed noon. The paddlers grew weary in the breezeless heat of late afternoon. Carol wet a handkerchief in the river to cool Stephen's head. Time slowed down and the Kronkel seemed to elongate as the sun lowered toward the horizon.

**

Standing in his canoe, Narai thrust the point of his paddle deep into a clump of elephant grass. Thus anchored, he sat down, gazing upstream. He reflected on the strange events of the past month… the riverboats… meeting Tuans on the "freeway"… Hadi and Er's trip… the first Sawi trading excursion… the return of a Tuan who built a home on the Kronkel… the landing of the airplane… the departure of the Tuan, who promised to return three days later with his family.

Or had they misunderstood the Tuan's sign language?

This was the third day. Three miles downstream all the villagers from Haenam and Kamur had gathered. Scouts like Narai speckled the Kronkel, ready to pass along any sign of the Tuans.

Time and the Kronkel drifted by.

Narai glanced at the sinking sun. Perhaps the Tuan who had appeared out of nowhere had decided to…

Suddenly, a flash of paddles from upstream caught Narai's attention. He loosened his paddle in the elephant grass. But still he waited. Finally, he caught a gleam of color among the Kayagar paddlers. A Tuan!

Narai stood up tall in his dugout and raised a bamboo horn to his lips. He blew out a long, low blast.

Other scouts relayed the signal to the villages of Kamur and Haenam. Narai, smiling excitedly, prepared to escort the Tuans to their destination.

***

Appearing as if by magic, a lone Sawi pulled up beside Don and Carol's dugout.

"Konahari!" Don called.

"Konahari!" the paddler replied, smiling.

Soon a second, then a third escort emerged from the blue haze of evening, skimming over the Kronkel. By the time the Richardsons reached the last bend, six or seven small canoes had formed a convoy. The occupants called out in their mysterious, flowing language, ending each sentence with a long, powerful "…ooooooooo!"

Carol and Don peered through the legs and paddles, trying to catch a glimpse of their new home. They were totally unprepared for what greeted their gaze.

Two hundred armed warriors mobbed the shore, their silhouettes glowing against the red-gold horizon. Feathers decorated their hair and fluttered from their spears. Farther back, near the recently constructed house, an equal number of women and children watched, exclaiming in hushed tones over the Tuans' strange appearance.

The paddlers grew silent as the canoe glided in and struck shore at the feet of the armed crowd.

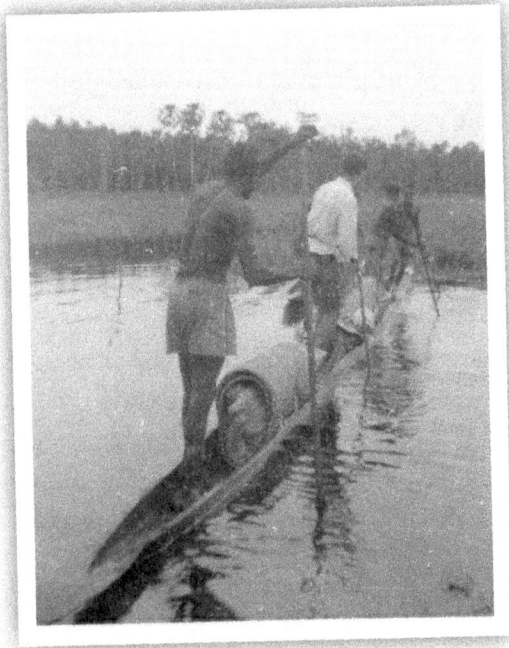

Don and two Sawi men paddle a dugout laden with supplies.

CHAPTER 11

A BAPTISM OF STRANGENESS

"Look at them!" Carol gasped.

Closer now, they could see the gruesome white and red-brown paint smeared on Sawi faces in such a way as to make their eye sockets look like gaping black holes. The spiny ridges of their spear barbs stood out in clear detail. Their excited whispering sizzled through the air.

Could they be the same people who only days before had gathered materials for Don's home? While working, it had been easy to forget these people were *still* headhunters and cannibals. Now they looked like it!

Don wondered if he had misunderstood. Were they expressing welcome, or was this something else? Had he missed God's leading in bringing his wife and son here so soon? Questions hammered Don's heart and head.

Some of the Sawi stepped into the water and gripped the sides of the dugout.

Have I been a fool, God? Don breathed in prayer. *These men have never learned to respect a policeman, let alone honor You—and here we are sixty-five river-miles from the nearest government post! We have nothing to protect us except Your Spirit.*

Is it only human pride, instead of Your peace, that has been keeping us going?

The Sawi drew the dugout onto the mud bank. God's peace flooded Don once again. But what about his family?

Stephen smiled happily at the fearsome warriors and reached toward them with his chubby arms. Carol moved out from under the dugout canopy to stand beside Don. Her face clearly showed excitement, with no anxiety marring it.

The Kayagar paddlers stepped warily ashore, clearing the way for Don and Carol.

Someone seized Don's arm. A wildly excited Hadi! Another hand gripped his shoulder. Nair! His one eye gleamed with a light of its own. Sawi women and children reached out to gently touch Carol and Stephen. They had never dreamed of beings so different from themselves.

Warriors pressed around Don and Carol so tightly that they could not move. They could only stand and wait to see what would happen.

Suddenly the whispering swelled into a cry of *Esa! Esa! Esa!* It was clearly a signal, but for what?

Alarmed at the sudden noise, Stephen looked up at his parents' faces for reassurance. Both had peace shining from their eyes. The baby relaxed.

But the test was not yet over.

Drums exploded around them, causing Don and Carol to jump, then shudder. Don saw one of the drums—thin-waisted, flared at both ends. Exotic designs decorated the drum body. A speckled lizard-skin drumhead stretched over the edges, glued on with human blood.

Warriors shouted and leaped into the air, jabbing their spears up and down. The shouts became chants, and the leaping turned into dancing. Wave after wave of warriors swirled closer, as if to envelope them. *It's like a baptism,* Don thought. *A baptism of strangeness.*

From somewhere beyond the noise and advancing twilight shadows Don felt like he could hear a voice. *Missionary, why are you here?*

Don had often answered that question when others asked. Now the Lord Himself asked it. Don thought about his earlier responses, deciding that none of them seemed right. Finally he found an answer.

Lord Jesus, it is for You we stand here, drenched not in water, but in Sawi humanity. This is our baptism into the work You planned for us before creation. May Your will be done among these people as it is in heaven. And if any good comes to them through us, the honor is Yours!

The Lord replied, *The peace of God, which passes all understanding, will guard your hearts and minds through Christ.*

***

The crowd swelled forward, pressing Don and Carol toward their new home. Together the Richardsons climbed up the steps of their porch. As they turned toward the crowd, a huge shout vibrated the air. Men and boys leaped up and down, drumming and chanting with vigor. Women danced behind, their grass skirts tossing like waves of the sea.

The warriors' faces shone with pleasure. They had not meant to frighten their guests. Rather, they were simply displaying their excitement over having Tuans in the village.

The six Kayagar paddlers managed to squirm through the crowd with the Richardsons' belongings. Don found a flashlight and led Carol into the house. The Sawi danced outside, shouting and stamping their feet.

Black crickets scuttled away from the flashlight beam as Don shone it around the house. A large green tree frog leaped frantically from one rafter to another. Dancers crowded onto the porch to inspect the Tuans.

Don pumped up the kerosene camp lantern and lit it. Startled Sawi immediately leaped off the porch onto the marshy ground. The drumming stopped as abruptly as a radio switched off and hundreds of feet stampeded away into the night. Don set down the lamp and went outside to reassure the Sawi.

Once outside, he saw why they had fled; the entire house looked like a gigantic jack-o-lantern! Bright light beams radiated out through every door and window and hundreds of cracks in the sago-frond walls.

"Don't be afraid! Come back!" Don called.

Slowly, Nair and the others returned—glad to see that the light came from some sort of tool and not from Don and Carol themselves. The drums began again. Dancers circled the house once more, but at a cautious distance.

Don spread out a bedroll in a corner and hung a mosquito net over it. Carol cooked a simple meal on the stove. Stephen, worn out from the excitement, fell asleep to the pounding of the drums.

"I'm not afraid, Don," Carol smiled. "I know that God has given me the ability to live here. He will do a great work! He wants Sawi to know Him!"

Don agreed. But he knew they would first have to learn the Sawi language before they could share the Good News.

CHAPTER 12

THE SAWI
SUPERMARKET

Nair's body tensed in his hide-out, and he pulled his vine bow-string taut. The long bamboo arrow peeked through a gap in the sago fronds. In the eerie moonlight he looked exactly like his ancestors who had hunted in these swamps for centuries.

Suddenly the arrow flew, skewering a wild boar eating sago pulp from a palm trunk Nair had split open as a trap. The boar shrieked and bolted away with blood pouring from its body. At the edge of the clearing it whirled to face its tormentor but could see no enemy. Then the pig collapsed, rolled on its side, and lay still.

Nair fitted a second arrow to his bow and cautiously approached the boar. He poked it with his foot, relaxing the bowstring when he saw it was dead.

He returned to his hide-out to retrieve six short sago fronds. He wove the leaves together to make carrying packs for his kill. Next Nair took a narrow bamboo razor from a bag, crouched over the carcass, and began the long task of butchering.

Moonlight lit the wings of hundreds of mosquitoes whining around him. Fireflies flickered among the liana vines. Patches of eerie light gleamed from rotting plants back in the jungle.

Nair's jungle.

He divided the carcass into three piles—meat, internal organs, and bone. He finished weaving the fronds closed around the food, then hoisted one sixty-pound pack onto his back. His sons would retrieve the others later.

Dawn broke over the swamplands. Nair gathered up his bow and the arrows, including the bloody one that had completely pierced the pig. It took a mighty hunter to send an arrow through a pig's body!

Yes, Nair looked just like his ancestors in every way. Except one.

Returning to the hide-out, Nair picked up the new steel machete he had earned by helping the Tuan build his home. He had used it to cut the fronds for his hide-out. This was the only change from his past, but it was a big one.

***

Two of Nair's four wives placed themselves on opposite sides of a tall sago palm and battered its trunk with stone axes from both sides until the fibers grew weak. The giant tree shook and crashed down, partially burying itself in the soft jungle mud.

The women pried off the outer layer of the trunk to reach the pulpy core, which they chopped out with stone tools. Then they washed the fibers in a trough, draining off their staple food—sago flour.

High overhead, one of Nair's sons clung to the topmost branches of a jungle tree, keeping watch in case some Asmat raiders looking for human heads were drawn by the sounds of chopping. He studied the flocks of cockatoos. If they acted uneasy, an enemy might be approaching. The Sawi often called the cockatoo "the revealer." The birds remained calm that day.

After washing about seventy pounds of sago flour in the trough, the women drained off the water and burned the outside of each doughy lump. The gooey coating hardened. They peeled off some of the hardened mass from a sago loaf, dividing it for a healthy mid-day snack.

Children had come from the treehouse for this special treat. They laughed as they stretched the rubbery food until it broke and snapped back into their hands. Their mothers smiled, wrapping the moist loaves of sago flour to carry home.

***

One of Nair's older sons, Amio, moved silently through the swamp glades under the eighty-foot sago palms. He leaped from one root formation to another, skirting the main pools.

The splash of a catfish caught his attention. He squatted on a root and waited by the pool, bow and arrow in hand. A second fish jumped, then a third. Amio stood to scan the trees around him.

Finally, he saw the tree he wanted. Pulling a new steel knife from his belt, Amio stripped several pieces of bark from the side of the tree. He carried the bark, oozing with a thick, white sap, to the side of the pool. Amio knelt down and rubbed the bark pieces together under the water.

A soft whiteness spread through the tea-colored pool. It sank slowly, like milk in coffee. Amio picked up his bow and fitted a fish-arrow to the vine-string.

Soon a fish rose to the surface, gasping with pain, its eyes clouded over with milky sap. Amio's arrow pierced its body. The fish thrashed around, still at the surface, dragging the arrow along. When it came within reach, Amio caught the end of the arrow and lifted his prey out of the water.

Several more blinded fish broke the surface. Amio caught them all. He made a sago-frond pack to wrap up the fish—after he removed the poisonous spines from their dorsal fins. He didn't want to put on a backpack only to feel a needle-prick! Amio loaded up the fish and headed home.

***

Two of Nair's daughters chatted softly as they walked carefully through the sago palms. They avoided the clumps of six-inch thorns that guard sago palm saplings. The girls reached the edge of a quiet pool and reached into the water. They lifted out several sago-frond sacks which they had placed there a few days before.

The sacks held baby leaves taken from the inside of a felled sago palm. As the water drained out, the girls removed wriggling freshwater shrimp hiding in the fibers of the trap. The girls lowered the traps back into the murky water. They skipped from pool to pool, collecting shrimp.

Once they finished that chore, they cut a path into the elephant grass, breaking off the stems just below water level. They stripped off the six-foot-long leaves, plucked out the center of each plant, and added them to their packs.

The girls headed back to their treehouse, stopping periodically to pick other edible leaves or to shake ripe fruit from trees. Occasionally they stooped to pull a leech from their feet or ankles, tossing it aside without a second thought.

***

The food-gatherers reached their treehouse home and stored their groceries in three dugouts. Today they would leave for the Tuans' village, so there was no need to haul the heavy packs up into the house.

The Sawi enjoyed a bountiful jungle supermarket! Besides pork, sago, fish, shrimp, elephant grass cores, edible leaves, and fruit,

Nair's family also added bundles of squirming beetle grubs and a death adder snake killed with an arrow by a child. Some of the youngest children had caught frogs and a lizard to contribute to the feast.

Grubs are harvested from the rotting trunk of a sago palm.

Nair's family climbed into the treehouse and chewed on roast pork while they listened to the story of how he had killed the boar. The one-eyed man held the boar's ear in his hands as he talked. A wood tick looking for a new home crawled from the ear onto his hand. Nair casually flicked it into the fire beside him, where it sizzled and popped.

Using a bamboo razor, Nair carved a circular piece of flesh out of the boar's ear. He cut a hole in the middle of this piece, then fitted the ring on the end of his bow with similar trophies of boars he had killed before.

Nair was a powerful bowman. He had four wives who lived at peace with him, eleven living sons and daughters, many grandchildren, and the dread of his enemies. What more did he need?

Nair looked down at his new machete, running a finger along its gleaming edge. What more *did* he need?

More machetes, axes, and knives, for sure. His own machete and Amio's knife were a start. Nair wanted each of his wives and children to possess at least a machete, an axe, and a knife. This would take time and work, for it was clear that the Tuan did not plan on giving these treasures away as gifts. Nair didn't mind. He and his family always worked hard.

But was there more? Nair sensed that the Tuan and his wife wanted to change something in the Sawi universe but he had no idea what or how. His curiosity burned—he had to know what the Tuans wanted!

"Let's go to Kamur!" he called, rising to his feet.

Nair's wives and children rolled up grass mats and sprinkled water from bamboo holders to extinguish the cooking fires. Memorial skulls of relatives were tied up in the rafters. Then the family began the long descent to the jungle floor.

Hours of paddling later, Nair approached the Tuans' home on the Kronkel. They could see smoke curling sleepily over the houses.

Suddenly Nair's one eye noticed that more than just smoke rose over the settlement. Shafts of white flashed like needles in the sun as they crisscrossed above the treetops before falling back to earth. Just then he heard shouting. And wailing.

"Hurry!" Nair called to his family. "There's a battle going on in the Tuans' yard!"

CHAPTER 13

WAR AT THE DOOR

"Carol!" Don shouted above the bedlam outside, "keep the baby away from the windows!"

Grabbing language notes, Don dashed toward the house, threading his way between armed men of Kamur. Don's language helper vanished into the jungle in the opposite direction.

Angry warriors from Haenam shot arrows toward their Kamur attackers. Three of them seemed to be falling toward Don, so he leaped behind his house, under the shelter of the roof. The arrows struck and quivered in a forty-foot circle around the small house. Not as close as he had expected.

Don hurriedly climbed the back steps. He glanced at Carol who was holding Stephen in the storeroom—the one room with an inside wall—then stepped to the front door to take in the scene.

Two lines of warriors faced each other across the open ground Don had cleared for his home. No one tried to hide behind anything. They preferred to fight in the open. Battle spears were thrust into the ground so the men had their hands free for their bows. Warriors rose to their full height to release arrows and then crouched down to provide a smaller target. Their attention was riveted on the battle. Arrows shot back and forth at more than one hundred miles per hour. Even a split second of inattention could prove deadly.

The more experienced warriors from each side lined up in the front, shooting and dodging from about fifty yards apart. The less experienced—mostly teenage boys—stood farther back and lofted their arrows high in the air so they would rain down from above. Each fighter had to watch out for arrows coming straight toward him as well as those showering down from the sky. As each man's arrows ran out, he simply plucked others up off the ground and shot them back.

Women lined the perimeter of the clearing, waving their sago-pounding sticks and shouting curses at their enemies. They either stamped their feet in rage or wailed in fear. Children climbed up on logs or stumps to see the fighting more clearly.

Warriors and spectators alike waited for the first arrow to strike human flesh. When a man was hit, all the fighters would concentrate their arrows to finish him. Don strode out on the front porch, ready for action, but unsure what to do.

This is real, he thought. *It's not a Hollywood movie. These men are really trying to kill each other. They may lose their lives before I've had a chance to tell them about Jesus.*

Do something! his mind shrieked.

Don opened his mouth to shout for the men to stop, but then hesitated. If he yelled, a fighter might be distracted just when an arrow came toward him.

Perhaps he should run into the fray waving his arms. Surely the Sawi would stop shooting then. They realized that not many Tuans waited to come in and take his place, didn't they? Then again, perhaps winning the battle meant more to them than having a Tuan around.

Advice Don had received earlier popped into his mind: "Be careful about trying to act the peacemaker—it takes only one arrow in the right place, and your ministry, if not your life, will be ended."

"True," Don thought. "These warriors know how to handle themselves among flying arrows. I don't. Probably if I just pray and wait no one will get hurt. Surely God doesn't expect me to jump in when I don't even know the langu…"

A mighty shout shook the area. The warriors of Haenam thought one of their arrows had hit a fighter from Kamur. Yet, at the last minute, he had avoided it by leaping up so the arrow passed under his thigh.

Blessed are the peacemakers, a voice within Don whispered, *for they shall be called children of God.* Don decided that peacemaking *was* one of his tasks—and why should he expect that job to be easy, painless, or riskless? Perhaps every true act of peacemaking had to involve risk for the peacemaker.

Don knew that the real battle wasn't between Kamur and Haenam. Rather, it was between savagery and the gospel of peace. Everything Don and Carol did spoke for what they believed. If he didn't get involved now, he would show that he did not plan to be involved in the future.

He leaped from the steps shouting one of the handiest of all Sawi words: "*Es!* Enough!"

Don bent low and prayed hard as he moved close to Kamur's end of the fighting—all the while waving at Haenam to stop shooting. The warriors on the close end of the line ceased firing. Taking courage, Don inched toward the center of the fighting.

God's strength rushed through Don, and his presence interrupted the flow of the battle. The shooting stopped. Shouting broke out all around. Men waved their bows in frustration. Don wondered how he would ever settle the cause of the fighting. He needed words—and Sawi words were what he did not yet have.

Suddenly a strong hand gripped Don's elbow. He looked down to see Nair's one eye looking up at him. Nair's chest heaved. He had just run from his canoe. *I'll take care of this*, his stern expression seemed to say.

Don sighed in relief as Nair strode past him and planted his feet firmly in front of the Kamur warriors. He turned his back fearlessly toward Haenam. What he yelled in Sawi was a mystery to Don, but the Kamur warriors lowered their weapons.

The men from Haenam, however, did not calm down. Don searched for someone to talk with them. He saw Hadi standing on a tree stump.

"Hadi!" Don shouted, searching for words in Sawi. "You…you *talk!*"

Stunned by Don's command, Hadi blankly stared back for several seconds before stepping down off the stump and successfully quieting the Haenam mob.

***

The Sawi prefer their villages separated by miles of empty swampland as a protective barrier. In their desire to be close to the Richardsons, Kamur and Haenam had agreed to live together. Villagers had replaced the dilapidated treehouses of the old Kamur settlement with new longhouses, built just 5 or 6 feet above the ground and swamp water. Kamur claimed the Tuans because they had built on Kamur land. Haenam claimed proximity rights because they had made first contact with Don on the Kronkel River through Hadi.

Joining two Sawi villages into one was an experiment only rarely tried. Such communal attempts usually ended in bloodshed. In this case, the excitement of living with two extremely rare beings thought to have a limitless supply of axes, machetes, knives, razor blades, mirrors, and who knew what else seemed enough to risk the venture. So, during the three days it had taken Don to gather up Carol and Stephen and return, the Sawi had also gathered up their families and returned.

The party atmosphere of the first few days had now vanished. Sawi attitudes could change quickly. The future of the new community did not look good. Don and Carol hoped to avoid bloodshed until they could learn the language. Perhaps then they could hold the two villages together in peace.

It turned out to be a vain hope.

CHAPTER 14

BLOODY HANDS

Curious Sawi boys crept toward the lighted window. Their eyes peered through cracks in the sago-frond walls—the only thing familiar about this house. Everything else, from the kerosene lamp to the shining yellow curtains, was totally alien. Counters, a table, chairs, tablecloth, plates, bowls, knives, forks, spoons, pictures on the wall, and a kerosene stove all puzzled the little swamp boys.

The boys watched the Tuan and his wife sit down to eat a meal with their baby. The boys' eyes widened in horror and fascination. Abruptly they fled from the porch, spreading an incredible report from house to house. The adults in the longhouses called back to them, "You must be mistaken!"

"Go quick and see for yourselves!" the boys cried.

Their curiosity intense, the adults rushed to Don's front porch. Don and Carol could see only the whites of their eyes shining in the blackness. The men did not respond to the Richardsons' greetings. Rather, they stared intently at the food on the table.

"It's true!" one of them exclaimed, his words unintelligible to Don and Carol. "The Tuan is eating brains!"

Wondering what all the excitement was about, Don lifted another forkful of macaroni noodles to his lips.

***

On another night, as Don turned off the lamp, he and Carol heard a woman crying out in anguish. He grabbed a flashlight and picked his way through the stumps and roots toward a Kamur longhouse.

"Why is that woman crying?" he called.

A man came to the doorway and waved Don away. "Why is that woman crying?" Don asked again.

Don only understood the last words of the man's reply: "Go away!"

Other villagers came to their doorways, shooing Don away. Feeling self-conscious at being unwelcome—as well as frustrated by his lack of language ability—Don headed home, none the wiser. From time to time he and Carol heard the woman cry out. Just before daybreak loud wailing from Kamur awoke them.

Later that morning they learned that the woman had died giving birth to twins. The babies also died. Even if the twins had lived, their own father would have killed one of them. The Sawi believed that the second twin born was actually an evil spirit trying to invade the community by pretending to be a human child. Demons could be anywhere in the Sawi world.

Don and Carol mourned with Kamur over the woman's death. They groaned with longing for the day when they would have the Sawis' trust to help even in such private matters as childbirth.

***

More problems arose in the village. A fight between two men who wanted to marry the same woman escalated to involve the suitors' friends and relatives. Mavu, who had already proved his deadliness when he joined Kani's legend-making revenge plot against Wasohwi village, was the first to strike. The fight lasted only seconds but left three men seriously injured.

When Don arrived Mavu was still raging, but there was no one left standing to answer his challenge. Seeing the severity of the fighters' injuries, Don called to Carol to help him clean and bandage the wounds. They worked together to stop the bleeding and prevent infection.

Don longed to say something to Mavu to make him think. He knew that scolding him for nearly killing his neighbors would only make Mavu shrug and spit, "So what?"

Instead, Don simply told Mavu, "You have made my wife's hands bloody."

This comment surprised Mavu. He winced, fearing that he might have committed some horrible act that would cause great changes in the spiritual world. Don longed to tell him of Someone else's hands that had been made bloody for his sake—and that truly did cause great changes in the spiritual world. But he didn't have the words. Not yet.

Carol set up a clinic to care for the Sawis' physical needs.

✳✳✳

Don and Carol gave the injured fighters injections of penicillin to prevent infection in wounds that might otherwise have proved fatal. A death would have caused a blood feud that could have continued for years. The Richardsons' sense of urgency for sharing the Good News deepened.

Don decided to spend ten hours a day studying the Sawi language. He worked with language helpers for three or four hours before visiting Sawi homes or manhouses for the rest of day, trying to enter into conversations. He and Carol learned by trial and error, as they had no dictionaries to clarify meanings or grammar books to explain structures. Slowly they gained confidence in the Sawi language and felt almost ready to share God's truth.

The Richardsons put off building a permanent home so they could focus on language study, deciding that a few improvements to their twenty-by-twenty-foot thatch house would make it livable enough, and that they could endure the armies of insects and other wildlife that found their way under, over, and through the walls. Cockroaches, flies, crickets, flying ants, moths, and mosquitoes constantly attempted to evict them, to no avail. They only succeeded in making Don and Carol go to bed early.

CHAPTER 15

MEETING IN THE MANHOUSE

Don approached the manhouse slowly, savoring the walk through the early morning puddles, drips, and glowing mist. He clutched his notes, watching the last clouds of an all-night rainstorm fade away over the ironwood trees. Today he planned to share about God.

What a struggle he'd had with language! Speaking Sawi was harder than he had imagined. Each verb had nineteen tenses and thirty-eight endings to choose from. But now that he had figured out many of the rules, he realized the language was remarkably efficient. The grammatical structure showed that its creators thought deeply and expressed themselves eloquently.

Don's ability to communicate was picking up rapidly. He finally felt ready to try sharing. He climbed into the Haenam manhouse and seated himself among the warriors. This was the main meeting house, into which only men were normally permitted to enter.

Gloomy-eyed skulls, weapons, grass mats, and flickering fires filled the room. While Don found many parts of Sawi life offensive, he also admired the Sawis' ability to live in their world. Each villager knew all the plants and animals of the jungle and could survive easily in the wilderness where Don, cut off from outside help, would waste away.

Sawis obviously had great courage and strong wills. They could move through rainstorms of arrows or face down a wild boar. They could even transform a seemingly hostile environment into a bursting supermarket with goods free for the taking—without destroying the land in the process.

Don shared two basic beliefs with the Sawi: a supernatural world existed all around them, and the interaction between that supernatural world and humans was supremely important.

The Sawi believed in a host of unfriendly, uncaring demons and spirits of the dead. Don trusted in an infinite, yet personal God who loves justice and mercy. The Sawi believed that nothing bad happened by accident, but was inevitably caused by demons. These demons could be controlled or stopped by witchcraft. Don was convinced that every event was either commanded or permitted by God, who invited human participation through prayer.

Beyond that point, there was little in common in their worlds. Don had to find some way this morning to meaningfully share with these people the hope that lived in his heart.

First, Don needed a word for God in Sawi. He chose "The Greatest Spirit." Next, Don tried to describe God. He explained that God didn't live in just one log or sago palm, like Sawi spirits, but instead filled the entire sky and earth. The Sawi glanced at one another, startled at the thought.

"In the case of your spirits," Don continued, "you use witchcraft to keep them from entering your villages, homes, or bodies. But there is no way to keep God away. He does not respect witchcraft. He is everywhere, and no one can ever get away from Him."

The Sawi looked around helplessly.

"And because everything—the sun, the moon, the weather, rivers, jungle, animals, and people—are all under His power, He knows everything. He knows what everyone is saying, doing, and thinking. We cannot see Him, but He sees us!

"He also controls everything, just as easily as you control the movements of your own muscles. Without Him the wind cannot blow, nor the rain fall. The sun cannot shine, nor the moon rise without His power. Neither could plants grow, nor babies be born."

Kani and the others leaned forward, listening intently. Up to this point they had only received goods from the outside world. Now they were receiving new ideas.

Line by line, Don contrasted the small, cruel Sawi spirits with the infinite, loving God. He spoke of God's love for justice and mercy as He sought to save lost men. Don told about God creating the world and placing men in a beautiful place. He shared the story of evil entering the world and the age-old promise of a Deliverer—then the coming of that Deliverer, Jesus. Right at the most exciting part, as Don spoke of Jesus' ministry among the Jews, Maum yawned and began fidgeting. He had stopped listening.

Others also returned to their own conversations. Don sensed that if he had been talking about the Asmat, Kayagar, or other groups, they would have kept on listening. But he had reached the end of their attention span. The Jews, whoever they were, sounded very far away.

On future visits to the Haenam manhouse Don told more stories about Jesus and His work, trying to show the Sawi that He mattered in their lives. They didn't seem to agree.

Only once did they show any enthusiasm for Don's stories of Jesus—when he described Judas Iscariot's betrayal. About halfway through the story, Don noticed that all the men were listening intently. They absorbed all the details: for three years Judas had kept close company with Jesus, sharing the same food, traveling the same road.

That any friend of Jesus would have thought of betraying such an important person was highly unlikely. And yet Judas, one of Jesus' highly trusted disciples, had chosen to betray Him and carried out the dreadful act alone, without any of the other disciples suspecting his plot.

At the peak of the story, Maum whistled a call of admiration. Kani and others touched their fingertips to their chests in awe. Others chuckled.

Don sat there confused. Then he realized, *they had identified Judas as the hero of the story!* Judas, who Don had described as an enemy of the truth, had become their role model.

They recognized Judas' treachery and revered it. Don didn't know yet that Maum and Kani had plotted the murders of Yae, Fusuman, and seven other visitors from Wasohwi.

Don shuddered as if a bucket of cold water had been poured over his head. He tried to protest, to tell them that Jesus was good. He was the Son of God, the Savior! To betray Him was evil. Yet nothing Don said erased the gleam of savage admiration from the Sawis' eyes.

"That was real *tuwi asonai man!*" Kani exclaimed.

Tuwi asonai man meant nothing to Don. He left the manhouse feeling hopeless and frustrated. Across the swamp he could see the little home he had built. Carol stood on the porch treating injuries and passing out medicine. Stephen played on a mat behind her. Was that all they could do? Bring health to physical bodies while ignoring spiritual death?

The Haenam warriors chuckled over Don's story as he walked away. At home Don shared his experience with Carol, and the two of them began to pray. As they prayed, Don kept hearing Kani's strange words.

Tuwi asonai man! The words were simple enough. *Tuwi* meant "pig." *Ason* meant "to catch," and with the *–ai* ending, "having caught." *Man* meant "to do."

"Having caught a pig, to do... to do what?" Don wondered.

He found one of his language helpers and asked what *tuwi asonai man* meant. The helper pointed through the window to a young pig which Nair had captured and tamed. It roamed freely around the village now.

"Tuan, when Nair first caught that pig, he kept it in his home, fed it by hand, and protected it from the village dogs. Now that it is roaming about, he still throws down scraps of food for it every day. The pig is secure, protected, and well-fed. He is free to come and go as he pleases. But one day when the pig is grown, what will happen to it?"

"Nair and his family will butcher it and eat it," Don replied.

"But does the pig have any warning now of that coming event?"

"Not the slightest," Don answered.

"Right! *Tuwi asonai man* means to do with a man as Nair is doing with that pig—*to fatten him with friendship for an unsuspected slaughter!*"

Don's helper watched the effect of his words on Don's expression.

"Does this really happen?" Don sputtered incredulously.

"Of course," he replied quickly, then told the story of Yae, who used to come to Haenam often. On his first visit he had been treated like a king and invited to return again and again. The story ended when Yae's "friends"—including Paha, Maum, and Kani—became his murderers, and Yae became the main course at a feast.

"Let me tell you about Kani and Paha, too," the helper continued. He told the story of their treachery against Paha's own family members from Wasohwi. Don sat in stunned silence.

"But if Paha did something that bad," Don said, "why is he so popular? Why have so many men promised their daughters in marriage to him?"

Don's helper didn't see the point of the question. That was an answer in itself.

Don started uncovering more tales of treachery and murder. He saw that the Sawi were not only cruel, but they *honored* cruelty. Their greatest satisfaction came from the misery and despair of others. Ordinary killing held less interest for them. They willingly let a victim escape in order to try *tuwi asonai man*.

No wonder they liked the story of Judas Iscariot so much. Judas was a super-Sawi! Jesus meant little to them.

The realization felt overwhelming. The Richardsons needed to completely change their perspective. Yet how could one missionary family change the worldview of an entire culture and a value system passed down for thousands of years?

Don knew that he couldn't just tell the Good News over and over in the same ineffective way. Nor was he willing to forget the adults and only concentrate on the children. He wanted to win *this* generation of Sawi, on their own terms, by their own cooking fires. Surely the gospel had the power to win men like Paha, Kani, Nair, and Kigo.

How could he share the truth in a way the Sawi would understand? Don was willing, but at a loss. *Lord,* he groaned, *in all of space and time has Your message ever found a worldview more opposite to the gospel? And has anyone ever faced a bigger communication problem than I have?*

John the Baptist had no problems communicating. The people he preached knew about baptism and repentance from sins. He talked about a Messiah coming to people who had waited years for His coming! The Jews knew all about lambs and offerings for sin. But the Sawi have never heard of lambs and they glorify sin!

Don continued praying, *The Greeks had words that could be used for Jesus like Logos, or "Word." But God, did you prepare the Sawi in any way for Your gospel? The Sawi don't even have a word for You! They don't have any ideas of You. Nothing that I can use!*

It seemed to Don that God had led him to the end of the earth and then abandoned him to struggle with a communication problem greater than anyone had ever experienced before. Or was Don misreading the situation?

Surely God's grace would find a way to break through to the Sawi, too. There must be a way—but what could it be? *Lord,* Don prayed, *I need Your help!*

***

Carol listened with concern as Don explained the problem. "Do you think there's any chance they're…" she faltered.

"…fattening *us* with friendship for a slaughter?" Don finished her thought. "It may have crossed their minds, but we are their only source of outside resources, and that probably helps us—at least for now. My main concern, though, is will the good news about Jesus ever break through this twisted way of thinking?"

"God always has a way," Carol answered confidently. "Let's trust that He'll show it to us."

Don agreed that if Jesus Himself were physically present in the manhouse, He would know what to say and do. But Jesus was not there physically. Only a man and a woman who hoped to be His representatives—who trusted that the Spirit of Jesus was alive and worked in them—were there with the Sawi. So the Spirit would have to show them what Jesus would say or do, or else there was no hope. Brought to complete dependence on God alone, Don and Carol decided to trust Him for an answer. They didn't know what form it would take.

The next day a fresh round of serious fighting broke out again between Haenam and Kamur.

CHAPTER 16

CRISIS BY THE KRONKEL

The Sawi began training children for war as soon as they learned to walk. Fathers encouraged their children to disobey commands to prove their "strong will." Violent temper tantrums were always rewarded. Young children who hadn't learned to swim would throw themselves into a river just to make a parent or sibling rescue them. If an adult physically punished a child (a rare occurrence among the Sawi), the child would often hit back. Parents accepted this reaction, encouraging more of the same behavior.

Sawi children were trained to get their way by the force of their tempers and physical violence. Parents pushed them to take revenge each time they received a hurt or insult. Children watched their relatives retaliate against everything that offended them. They listened to stories and legends which glorified violence and treachery.

After sixteen to eighteen years of such training, Sawi young men had a fighting instinct so deeply ingrained that even concern for their own safety couldn't overcome it. It did not surprise Don and Carol, then, that whole villages of such men would bristle with spears and arrows at a word or glance, including Kamur and Haenam.

Don and Carol counted fourteen battles in their front yard during the first two months they lived with the Sawi. After that, they stopped counting. It seemed that if the Sawi developed modern weapons, they would destroy half the earth!

***

Someone would surely be killed soon. A long blood-feud would inevitably follow between Haenam and Kamur. Don pleaded with the leaders of both villages to make peace, but they replied, "Tuan, you just don't understand!"

One day a new thought stopped Don in his tracks. He had been assuming that peace was possible. Peace, however, requires assurance of goodwill on both sides. Among the Sawi, where *tuwi asonai man* was always a possibility, could there ever be an assurance of goodwill? Each side knew perfectly well the other's love of treachery.

When treachery and betrayal were acceptable, lasting peace appeared impossible. Long, long ago, the ancestors of the Sawi had trapped the entire culture in an endless cycle of war. Don wanted to help them break the cycle, but he could see no way to do it.

At times, Don wondered to himself why there were any Sawi left alive. With only half of their babies surviving to adulthood and those who did likely to die before the age of twenty-five, the Sawi could hardly afford to kill each other. Yet they were intent on doing just that!

Don concluded that their practice of living in small, separate groups was the key to their survival. Potential enemies remained far apart, so they had fewer chances to kill one another. Diseases also spread more slowly when the villages were scattered. They depended more on one another and valued each other more highly in their small communities.

Don realized that he and Carol had unintentionally taken away the isolation Kamur and Haenam had long relied on to survive. The Richardsons contemplated that, for the good of the people, they may have to leave.

That thought was a bitter pill to swallow, but they knew that without Tuans, Haenam and Kamur would scatter to their deep jungle homes and live in relative peace. Perhaps Don and Carol could try to reach other Sawi communities in the area or a neighboring tribe that would more readily accept their message.

After praying with Carol about their decision, Don went to talk with the leaders of Kamur and Haenam.

"Since you cannot make peace with each other," he announced sorrowfully, "it seems clear that we must leave you. If we stay here, more lives will be lost and you will be locked in a never-ending revenge cycle. We will go to other Sawi villages on a different river. Perhaps they are living at peace."

Don's words set off a thunderstorm of discussion in the two man-houses. He trudged home. A sense of loss and concern grew as he thought of Carol, pregnant with their second child, having to move to a new jungle home, and of Stephen, ill with malaria, growing pale and sickly.

Later that night, Don heard a shout outside his back door. His flashlight beam played across faces from both warring groups—Kani, Paha, Maum, Nair, Kigo, and others.

"Tuan," one of them pleaded, "don't leave us!"

"But I don't want you to kill each other," Don responded.

"Tuan, we're not going to kill each other." The speaker paused, gulped, then blurted out, "Tomorrow, Tuan, we are going to make peace!"

CHAPTER 17

COOL WATER TOMORROW

"Make peace?" Don echoed unbelievingly. The speaker had actually blurted out, "Tomorrow we are going to sprinkle cool water on each other!"

"Cool water," in the Sawi language, meant "peace."

Don wondered if he had correctly interpreted Sawi culture. According to his understanding, the Sawi could not possibly reach anything more than what could be called a tie. Unless, of course, one side dumbly trusted the other completely—not very likely given the history he had learned! Either the leaders were lying about their intentions tomorrow, or Don had an incomplete understanding. He prayed it was the latter! Don wondered what in the world the Sawi could do in order to prove their sincerity and rule out the possibility of *tuwi asonai man*.

The Richardsons barely slept that night, wondering what would happen the next day. They heard voices murmuring in their Sawi neighbors' houses far into the night.

***

Dawn brought back color and life to the jungle, river, and longhouses. Don and Carol watched out the window as Paha and his oldest wife climbed down from their longhouse in Haenam, heading toward Kamur. Paha carried one of his sons on his back. His wife, Syado, was sobbing. Other Haenam villagers also climbed down and watched silently.

Don and Carol moved onto their porch for a better view. Kamur villagers flocked down from their longhouses. The tension grew as hundreds of eyes, including those of the Richardsons, followed stoic Paha and weeping Syado.

Don and Carol could see grim determination on Paha's face. The child he carried seemed unaware of anything unusual. Carol gripped Don's arm in apprehension.

Syado looked over Paha's shoulder at the Kamur villagers, gathered and waiting with anticipation. Syado trembled violently, either from fear or sorrow. Suddenly she wrenched her son from Paha's shoulders. She ran back toward Haenam, screaming and clutching the little boy.

Paha raced after her, vainly trying to pull the child from her arms. Syado clung to her baby with a mother's protective strength. Giriman, Paha's oldest son, raced to his father and prevented him from taking back the child. Paha stalked back and forth in front of the people of Haenam shouting words Don and Carol didn't understand.

Obviously, Syado and Giriman had interrupted whatever Paha had meant to do. All the other women of Haenam clutched their children close to their hearts, crying out in fear and worry. Men ran back and forth, shouting and pointing. The village boiled like a disturbed ants' nest.

A shout from Kamur drew the Richardsons' attention. Something was happening in the center of the village. Don left Carol on the porch and ran to a better place to see. A man named Sinau raised a baby boy over his head for all to see. Then, his face broken with terrible pain, Sinau handed the child to his brother, Atae. "I can't bear to give him over myself!" Sinau cried. "You do it for me!"

Atae took the baby and strode confidently toward Haenam. Sinau, the father, could not turn away from his baby.

Suddenly, eyes spilling tears, Sinau leaped toward the child, shouting, "I've changed my mind! I can't let him go!" Sinau snatched his son from Atae's arms. The shouting swelled in both villages.

The tension in the air fairly crackled around Don. The hair on his neck began to crawl as he watched both villages in utter turmoil, struggling to complete some plan that they couldn't quite bear. Out of the corner of his eye, Don noticed a Kamur man named Kaiyo turn away from the crowd and quickly climb up into his longhouse.

***

Kaiyo's heart pounded as he slipped away from his wife, Wumi, and ran up the ladder to his home. Paha had failed! Sinau had failed! Both Paha and Sinau had many children, yet neither of them could bring himself to give even one.

Kaiyo had only one child, six-month-old Biakadon, sleeping on the floor of the longhouse. Kaiyo approached his son. His heart broke at the thought of what he was about to do. Biakadon stirred and smiled sweetly at his father. He wiggled his little brown fists in the hope of being picked up.

"It must be done," Kaiyo reminded himself. "There's no other way to stop the fighting. And if the fighting does not stop, the Tuan will leave."

Kaiyo picked up his son and held the soft, warm body close to his chest one last time. He knew he would bring great grief to his wife, but there was no other way. Kaiyo headed toward the door on trembling legs, his face a mask of grief and determination.

***

Wumi, Biakadon's mother, stood in the middle of the jostling, shouting crowd, wondering with all the rest whether there would be peace. Of course, if anyone could bring himself to the point of handing over a child, it would be someone who had many children and therefore wouldn't miss one of them too badly. It was out of the question that she and Kaiyo would consider giving Biakadon.

But, she wondered, a cold finger of dread circling her heart, *where is Kaiyo?* He had been beside her just a few moments before. Wumi glanced toward the longhouse just as Kaiyo leaped down from the ladder at the far end and began running toward Haenam—with their son in his arms!

Frozen with shock and disbelief, Wumi stared like a statue. Kaiyo had their son! He was headed toward Haenam! Wumi screamed, then sprinted after Kaiyo, pleading with him to stop.

Kaiyo never looked back. He raced ahead of Wumi. In her desperate rush, Wumi slipped off the trail and fell into a wet bog. With no hope of catching Kaiyo she collapsed into the mud, wailing uncontrollably, "Biakadon! Biakadon, my son!"

***

Don glanced at Carol who was holding Stephen tightly. They both felt Wumi's anguish as they imagined the pain of losing a child.

Two other emotions overwhelmed Don. The first was anxiety. What fate awaited little Biakadon? Don tore his gaze from Wumi and followed Kaiyo toward Haenam. He decided that if Biakadon's life were in danger he would use every power he possessed to rescue him and return him safely to his mother.

The second emotion was intense curiosity. What were these people doing? Why was it necessary? The depth of Wumi's sorrow showed Don that she had lost Biakadon forever. Whatever purpose Kaiyo had, it could not be reversed.

***

Kaiyo's chest heaved with emotion as he reached the edge of Haenam. The leaders of the village stood in front of him, eyes fastened greedily on the child in his arms.

Kaiyo sought one face in the row of enemies before him. Finally, he spotted him and called, "Mahor!"

Mahor stepped forward, his eyes bright with emotion. The two men approached each other. All the Haenam villagers crowded closer, faces filled with anticipation. Behind him, Kaiyo heard a roar of excitement from the people in his own village who watched from a distance.

"Mahor!" Kaiyo challenged. "Will you plead the words of Kamur among your people?"

"Yes!" Mahor vowed, "I will plead the words of Kamur among my people!"

"Then I give you my son and with him my name!" Kaiyo cried, holding out Biakadon. Mahor gently took the child. Then he shouted, "It is enough! I will surely plead for peace between us!"

Both villages broke into thunderous shouting. The earth shook under their feet.

Paha suddenly reappeared in the front of the crowd at Haenam. He held another of his baby sons up and cried, "Kaiyo! Will you plead the words of Haenam among your people?"

"Yes!" cried Kaiyo.

"Then I give you my son and with him my name!" Paha placed the little boy, Mani, in Kaiyo's arms. A cry of despair sounded from the back of the crowd as close relatives of Mani realized what had just happened.

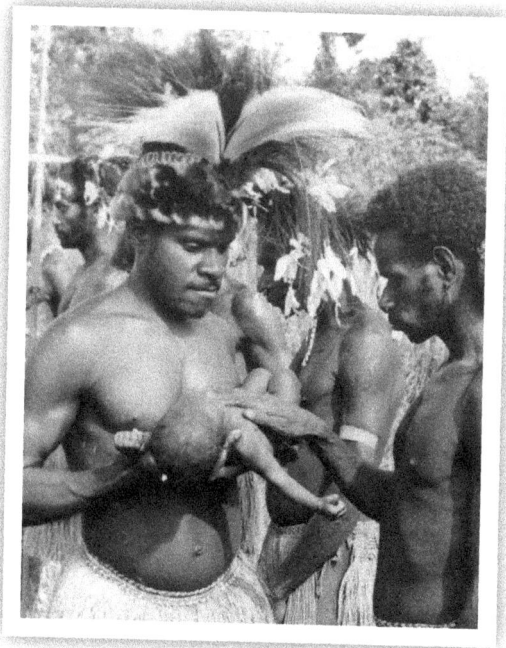

The exchange of the peace child
(from the Peace Child *film)*

Kaiyo was about to respond when Paha urged him, "Go! Go quickly!" Kaiyo raced back to Kamur with the baby. Mani's relatives tried in vain to overtake him.

As Kaiyo fled, Mahor shouted an invitation to all the people of Haenam. "Those who accept this child as a basis for peace, come and put your hands on him!"

Young and old, men and women, all filed eagerly past Mahor and placed their hands on tiny Biakadon, showing they accepted peace with Kamur. The same ceremony took place in Kamur as soon as Kaiyo returned.

The two babies were carried into the manhouses in their newly adopted villages. Loving hands decorated them for a peace celebration. Don saw no weapons as he walked among the crowds. He pulled one of the young men, Ari, aside to ask him what had just happened.

"Kaiyo gave his son to Haenam as a peace child, and Paha has given his son in return as a peace child to us!" Ari exulted.

"But why?" Don asked, puzzled.

"Tuan," he explained patiently, "you're the one who has been telling us we had to make peace. Don't you know that it's impossible to have peace without a *peace child*?"

Feeling very ignorant indeed, Don shook his head, bewildered.

"You mean, Tuan," Ari asked incredulously, "that you Tuans are able to make peace without...?"

He paused a moment, deep in thought. Suddenly his face brightened with understanding. "Oh!" he exclaimed. "I understand now.

You Tuans never war with each other, so of course you don't need a peace child."

Somewhere deep in Don's mind a tiny bell began ringing. God was trying to show him something. But the bell sounded very distant. Don barely noticed it.

The voices of dancers rang out loud and clear—and joyful—above the beating of drums. After six months of tension, horror, and violence, Don had almost forgotten how to feel cheerful. Yet how could he feel joy when Wumi, Kaiyo, and Paha had gone through so much anguish? "Tuan, you don't understand…" they had warned.

If Don had known that his call for peace would make fathers give up their own sons, cast mothers into grief, and throw babies into strangeness, would he have still chosen peace? He didn't know.

What he did know was that three hundred Sawi had placed their hands on a peace child. And those people were now singing and laughing. Inside Don the bell rang just a bit louder.

"What will happen to Biakadon and Mani?" Don asked Ari. "Will they be harmed?" Don felt uneasy, wondering if the joy of these unpredictable people might just be a celebration before a human sacrifice.

"They will not be harmed," Ari assured him. "In fact, both our villages will guard the lives of these peace children even more carefully than they protect their own children. If Biakadon and Mani die, then the peace will be broken."

That news both relieved and concerned Don. He felt happy knowing that nothing would happen to the babies through sacrifices or mistreatment. Yet he also felt concern because so many babies died early in life. A fall in the river, a bite from a poisonous snake, a sudden attack of a jungle disease, and the peace just purchased at such a cost would disintegrate.

Don pondered how peace depended on the continuing life of the peace child. The bell in Don's mind gave an extra loud ring—almost loud enough for him to notice.

***

The babies, adorned with armbands and leg-bands of braided vine, were carried out of the manhouses in the arms of the leading women of each village. The women faced each other from about fifty yards apart.

Men and boys from both Kamur and Haenam swarmed past their new peace child and met their former enemies halfway between the two villages. Smiles wreathed each face. The men exchanged gifts of axes, machetes, knives, shells, or necklaces of animal teeth. Those who exchanged gifts also exchanged names, effectively becoming members of the other village.

A dance followed the gift exchange. The men of Kamur gathered in a tight group while the men of Haenam whirled around them in a circle. Then the men of Haenam spun off to one side and stood together as the men of Kamur circled them.

Don called the dance the "you-in-me-I-in-you" dance. It showed the acceptance of peace between the two villages. That bell deep in Don's mind clanged louder and louder, impatient for him to realize what God was showing him.

As the celebration finished, Don called his language helpers over to learn more about what had just occurred.

Don had thought that the Sawi culture had just one main principle—an idealization of treachery and violence. Peace could never be achieved because no one could ever completely trust another. The theory seemed logical. Yet somewhere in the beginnings of the Sawi culture, the ancestors found a way to do what the theory said could not be done. They had found a way to prove their sincerity and establish peace.

If a man would actually give his own son to his enemies, that man could be trusted! That, and that alone, was proof of goodwill that no one could doubt.

Everyone who laid his hand on the child promised to not harm those who gave him. The bell clanged once more and finally caught Don's attention. He gasped as understanding flooded his mind. This was the key he and Carol had been praying for!

CHAPTER 18

GOD MUST HAVE BEEN SAD

A Sawi child gleefully jumped down from the branches of some trees into the river. He splashed into the water, soaking his companions who burst out in laughter. Don smiled as he approached the Haenam manhouse, notes in hand.

Two months of peace, he reflected. The peace child system worked!

Once it appeared that the peace might be broken. A Kamur pig had been mysteriously killed. The owner thought someone in Haenam had done it. He stormed off toward Haenam, ready to take revenge. Kaiyo suddenly stepped in.

Kaiyo had received the peace child from Haenam, so he had the right to settle problems between the two villages. He reached out toward the angry man and grabbed him by the earlobes, forcing him to stop and listen.

"If the peace child had died, you would be free to do what you want to do. But he is not dead," Kaiyo reasoned. "He is still alive. I am here representing Haenam in our village. You may not fight against them!"

Kaiyo pulled on the aggressor's earlobes again and he quietly walked back home! Later Kaiyo investigated the pig's death. Both villages eventually decided that the pig had been killed by a spy from another village that was angry with Kamur.

A living peace child could stop violence in Sawi villages. Don realized that the Sawi culture depended on *two* basic principles. Treachery was one of their foundational beliefs, but when the people tired of it, they relied on the other: a peace child.

***

Don seated himself among the men of the Haenam manhouse. "You saw how horrified I was when Kaiyo gave his son, Biakadon, to you," he began. "When I saw Wumi rolling in the mud, filled with such grief, I was almost ready to rush in among you, grab Biakadon, and give him back to his mother."

Paha, Mahor and others sat in silence, following Don's line of thought.

"I kept saying to myself, 'Oh that they could make peace without this painful giving of a son!' But you kept telling me, 'There is no other way!'"

Don leaned forward, pressing his hands against the sago-frond floor. "You were right!"

Every eye in the manhouse focused on him.

"When I stopped to think about it, I realized you and your ancestors are not the only ones who know that peace requires a peace child," Don continued. "God, the Spirit whose message I bring you, also said the same thing. True peace can never come without a peace child! Never!

"Because God wants men to find peace with Him and with each other, He decided to choose a once-for-all peace child good enough and strong enough to make peace, not just for a while, but forever! The problem was, whom should He choose? For among all human children, there was no son good enough or strong enough to be an eternal peace child."

Don paused, searching the men's faces. They were curious.

"Who did He choose?" asked Paha.

Don replied with a question of his own. "Did Kaiyo give another man's son, or his own?"

"He gave his own," they replied.

"Did you, Paha, give another man's son, or your own?" Don persisted.

"I gave my own," he whispered, remembering his anguish.

"So did God!" Don exclaimed. "Like Kaiyo, God had only one Son to give, and like Kaiyo, He gave Him anyway! The child you gave, Paha, was precious to you—not one you wanted to get rid of. Mani was your beloved son. God also gave His beloved Son!

"You respect words passed down from the ancestors. Hear what our ancestors say about the Peace Child from God."

Don opened his English Bible and translated part of Isaiah's prophecy into Sawi: "For to us a child is born, to us a son is given, and the government will be on his shoulders. And he will be called Wonderful Counselor, Mighty God, Everlasting Father, Prince of Peace" (Isaiah 9:6).

Don turned to the book of John next. "For God so loved the world that he gave his one and only Son, that whoever believes in him shall not perish but have eternal life" (John 3:16).

The Sawi men leaned forward, gazing at the strange cluster of white leaves in Don's hands, amazed by the message trapped inside that Don could set free.

Paha asked, "Is He the one you've been telling us about? Jesus?"

"He's the very one!" Don exclaimed.

"But you said a friend betrayed Him—if Jesus was a Peace Child, it was very wrong to betray Him. That's the worst thing anyone could do!"

"You're right again," Don answered, looking Paha in the eye. "Despising and betraying the Peace Child of God *is* the worst thing anyone could do."

Don watched the men's faces change. Before this moment Judas had been a super-Sawi. Now he was a villain.

"Tell us more," Paha urged.

Don talks with a Sawi friend.

***

A few hours later Don repeated the same message in Kamur's manhouse.

"When you, Kaiyo, gave Biakadon, it was to make peace with just *one* village—Haenam. Paha gave you Mani to make peace with just *one* village—your own. But Jesus is not a Peace Child for just one village. He is the Peace Child for *all* people—not only for Tuans, but for Asmat, Kayagar, and Sawi!

"You were very careful, Kaiyo, choosing the man to whom you would give your only son. You chose the one you thought would do the best job raising him. But when God searched for a man worthy to receive His Peace Child, He found no one! None of us was worthy. So did God say, 'I cannot give My Son because they are all unworthy'?"

Solemn faces studied Don through the wisps of smoke from cooking fires. Finally, Don answered his own question.

"No, He did not. He actually said, 'I will give Him anyway.'"

Don focused on Kaiyo. "Kaiyo, suppose someone had told you that when you gave Biakadon, the people of Haenam would treat him terribly—and even kill him. Would you still have given him?"

"Certainly not!" Kaiyo snorted.

"But in the case of Jesus," Don continued, "God knew beforehand that men would be cruel to Him and even kill the Peace Child He sent."

Kaiyo's face showed awe and disbelief as he anticipated the next words. "But God loves us so much that He gave His Son freely— even knowing men would despise and kill Him. In fact, through

God's wisdom, the men who killed Jesus actually provided the way to take away God's anger against people.

"They killed Him with evil thoughts in their hearts. Yet, God was so very clever that even the most terrible thing humans could do still accomplished God's purposes! If it had not been so, there would be no hope for any of us."

Just as Don was ready to tell of Jesus' resurrection from the dead, Nair let out a moan of deep sorrow.

Amio, Nair's son, explained. "Not long before you came, my father gave a peace child to the Kayagar. They took the baby but did not give one in return. Later we heard they killed my little brother and ate him."

Don drew his breath sharply in horror. He reached out and touched Nair's hand in mute sympathy.

Amio continued, "We learned then that Kayagar do not accept peace by placing their hands on a living peace child, like we do. Instead, they actually eat the peace child's body. That way an accidental death of the child does not end the peace, because he still is living inside everyone."

Don sat in stunned silence.

Then Nair whispered, "God must have been sad just like me."

***

Don continued sharing the same message of peace in the man-houses of other Sawi villages. "You can receive God's Peace Child by welcoming His Spirit into your hearts," he explained. "He then becomes your Provider and Protector. You will receive a new name. God will accept you because of Jesus."

The Sawi discussed these new ideas. Don pointed out to them that their own peace children, who were weak, brought peace. How much greater would the peace be that God's perfect Peace Child would bring?

"It's true," one man recounted. "Our peace children are not strong! I once knew a man who gave his son as a peace child to his enemies. He waited a few days before visiting the village which had received his child. The men stormed out of the manhouse, threatening him with spears.

"He cried, 'Why do you threaten me? I gave you my son!'

"They answered, 'Your son died last night! What are you doing here?' Then they killed him!"

The Sawi men rubbed their elbows, meaning that they were asking themselves, "What should we do?"

Don saw that he had not only discovered a parallel between their culture and the gospel, he had also pointed out that their own peace child was never enough. The Sawi knew that the peace child concept was the best they had. Now they realized, *man's best is not enough*. Only God can provide true peace.

CHAPTER 19

CAPSIZED AMONG CROCODILES

Over the next few months Don continued teaching about the Peace Child of God, inviting any who wanted to live by God's standard of peace to receive Him. The Sawi listened carefully, even longingly, yet no one expressed a decision to believe.

What held them back? It was their fear of a negative reaction from the demon world. How would the spirits view this unheard-of movement away from tradition? If the demons reacted angrily—and the Sawi were certain they would—could the Tuan and his God protect them from disaster? True, Don's reasons for receiving God's Peace Child rang true, but what would happen if they followed? No one had enough courage to take the leap.

Don wondered, "What else will it take to bring these men and their families to Jesus? I used the key that God prepared for them.

They understand about faith. But something more is needed. What else is there?"

Little did Don realize what God had in store for the Sawis—or what it might cost him to bring it about.

***

A few months after the peace child exchange, Don, Carol, and Stephen welcomed a new baby boy, named Shannon, into their family. When Shannon was two weeks old they packed a picnic lunch and set out to enjoy a day on the river together in their new dugout powered by an eighteen-horsepower outboard motor. Don had asked Nair, Maum, and Kani to make a keel for the canoe to help it travel more securely in the water. Miri, a young Sawi, joined the Richardsons as their river guide. He sat well forward in the bow of the three-foot-wide dugout, watching for any dangers.

"If you see any logs, Miri," Don said, "wave to me."

Miri nodded, but his eyes widened in fear as the boat raced forward over the smooth, black surface. They were traveling three times faster than Miri had ever gone before!

Ten minutes later, while cruising around a jungle-walled bend, Miri looked back and signaled frantically. Don reacted by swinging the canoe a bit too sharply to the left.

The dugout began to roll. The keel was not enough to stabilize them. Don tried to regain balance by swinging back to the right, but it was too late. Through one eternal second of horror he watched Carol, clutching newborn Shannon in her arms, disappear under the surface…Stephen fell into the black depths… Miri vainly leaned against the side of the dugout, attempting to right it…

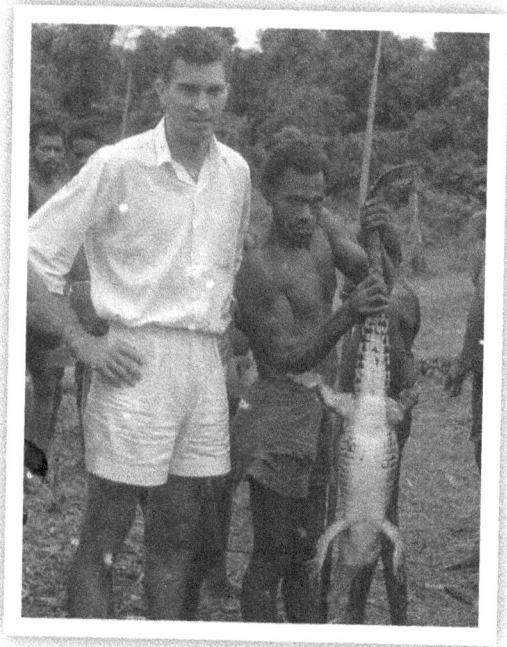

Don and a Sawi man with a crocodile
captured from the river

Then Don hit the water, still gripping the handle of the outboard motor, as the canoe finally capsized. He heard the muted roar of the engine throbbing under the surface—its propeller spinning dangerously close to his shoulder. Then the motor died, leaving them drifting in silence in the center of the crocodile-infested Kronkel River.

Miri surfaced immediately and reached for the keel. Fearing the crocodiles, he scrambled on top of the dugout and sat in a stupor. Carol, Stephen, and Shannon were nowhere in sight.

God help me! Don prayed in desperation. He had to find them before the current pulled them apart. Or before a crocodile attacked! That second thought jarred him into action.

Don couldn't see more than a few feet through the algae-stained water. He swam to the spot where Carol had disappeared, groping in all directions with his arms and legs.

Suddenly Shannon's face broke the surface right in front of him. Don grabbed him and thrust him up to Miri. Shannon immediately let out a loud, startled cry. *Good,* Don thought. *He doesn't have water in his lungs.*

Carol surfaced next. Don caught her wrist, pulling her close to the dugout. But where was Stephen?

Don frantically scanned the surface for some sign of his oldest son. He saw only reflections gleaming back from the water. And under the surface—blackness. Somewhere in the murk his nineteen-month-old was struggling, perhaps sinking toward the bottomless ooze of the Kronkel's bed twenty feet below. Don reached out again with his arms and legs. Nothing.

Father in heaven, keep the crocodiles away! he prayed. Then the thought flashed through his mind that Miri might be able to see through the reflections on the water from his vantage point on top of the dugout. "Miri!" he called, "Can you see Stephen?"

The question seemed to jolt Miri out of his daze. He scanned the surface carefully, then pointed at the water. Don swam that direction and spotted a tiny blur of blondness, faintly visible through the Kronkel's murky water. A second later he grabbed hold of Stephen. God, in His mercy, had given Stephen the sense to hold his breath under water. He was crying but unhurt. Don gratefully pushed him up to Miri on top of the dugout.

Now, how to get to shore? Should they abandon the canoe and swim with the two babies? Or try to right the dugout and bail it out, which would take at least ten minutes—and would the crocodiles wait that long? Or the fourteen-foot pythons?

If only someone were near with a canoe, Don thought desperately. *No chance,* he figured, *since there's only an hour of daylight left. No one will be this far from the village!*

God help us! came the anxious cry from his heart. Then he heard it. Frantic paddling. A Sawi dugout piloted by Miri's own father swung into view!

A minute later he floated beside the Richardsons, helping Carol into his dugout. Miri passed over Stephen and Shannon.

Don and Miri then righted the capsized canoe and began bailing it out. Miri kept looking fearfully at Don.

Paddling against the current, they all reached home just before dark, shivering from the dampness of their clothes and the thought of their near escape from tragedy. Sawi villagers lined the shore, anxious to learn what had happened.

Don began to tell about the accident, taking the blame for the whole thing. No one would listen. The Sawi turned on Miri, insulting and threatening him for being so careless with the Tuan and his family. That was why Miri had been so fearful. Capsizing a canoe was regarded as a serious crime among the Sawi. Miri cowered in front of Nair and the other leaders as they raged against him.

"Tuan!" Nair called angrily. "Just say the word and I'll thrash him for you with this length of vine!"

Don put his arm around the boy's trembling shoulders. Looking into Nair's one eye, he calmly replied, "None of you will raise a hand against my friend, Miri. Without his help, I could easily have lost one of my children in the river. As long as I live, Miri will be like a beloved son to me!"

The Sawi's astonishment showed plainly on every face. Don continued, "Instead of blaming Miri, join me in thanking God for saving us from tragedy!"

Nair dropped his whipping vine and bowed his head. The others followed his example. Don poured out his gratitude to God in the Sawi language. When he looked up, he saw Miri watching him, tears in his eyes.

✳✳✳

The following Sunday, Don spoke to a large gathering of Sawi and Atohwaem villagers on the theme of "Christ our Sinbearer." After the meeting, a young Atohwaem named Yodai came up. He had been listening to the Good News for several months.

He announced to Don, "I am ready to trust in Jesus who came from God!" Rejoicing, Don took him aside and taught him how to pray. Miri watched from a distance.

The joy on Yodai's face filled Miri with a strange envy. He wanted that joy, no matter the consequences. That same evening he asked to talk to Don. A few minutes later, Miri headed home throbbing with joy. He had entered the kingdom of God!

***

In May 1963 the Dutch government gave control of Netherlands New Guinea to the United Nations, with transfer to the Indonesian government to follow eight months later. This political event had a staggering impact on the Sawi and other tribes like them.

The Dutch government had basically left the wilderness areas untouched and uncontrolled. They had established a few widely scattered outposts, but didn't develop the area. As a result, the Sawi were relatively undisturbed.

The Indonesian government, however, took a very different approach. Teachers came to establish accredited schools in the national language. Police patrols increasingly enforced civil law. The harvesting of ironwood and other valuable timbers began in earnest. Crocodiles were hunted to near extinction for their highly prized skins. Western oil and copper mining companies constructed massive bases in the pristine wilderness. Roaring diesel generators, clattering helicopters, and thundering dynamite soon drowned out the jungle sounds.

Over time, migration of people from overcrowded Indonesian islands, particularly Java, turned the Sawi and their eight-hundred-thousand fellow New Guineans into a minority people in their own land.

What would have happened to the Sawi if the missionaries hadn't arrived first? Missionaries came to give the Sawi the Christian hope of eternal life and a belief system strong enough to support them as they catapulted from the stone age to the twentieth century. God cared enough about the Sawi to make sure they had a chance to hear the Good News first.

CHAPTER 20

MY LIVER TREMBLES

While Don rejoiced in Yodai and Miri's decisions, they were both young men, by no means leaders of their tribes. In order to transform the culture of the Sawi, the leaders needed to respond. Don wondered when that would happen, not knowing he didn't have long to wait.

He had just finished telling once more about the greatness of God's Peace Child, gently inviting any who wanted God's peace to receive Him when…

"Tuan Don!" Nair rose, facing Don squarely. He folded his arms in the manner of a leader. His chest heaved with emotion. Tiny muscles flexed along his jaw. His single eye gleamed like a hot coal through the smoke and shadow of the manhouse.

From early childhood, relatives had drummed into his head and heart the Sawi fear of eating, drinking, thinking, saying, or attempting anything that had not been blessed by the ancestors. To do so would make you "foolhardy." Some had called Nair foolhardy when, along with Kigo and Numu, he had chosen to stand and face the Dutch riverboats three years earlier.

But the decision he was about to announce now in the manhouse seemed to him far more daring. If they called him foolhardy when he chanced a mere physical meeting with the unknown, how much more so now!

Nair, his voice low and determined, proclaimed, "Your words make my liver tremble," meaning, *You have filled me with longing.* His voice cracked with a mixture of dread and purpose as he continued, "I want to receive the Peace Child of God!"

Don laid a hand on his shoulder. Nair seemed not to notice. His one eye gazed past Don, shining with radiance. There was no mistaking it—Nair was filled with spiritual joy.

"Has He come in?" Don whispered.

"He has come in!" Nair exulted. "It is Jesus! If He could give you peace even when your two sons almost drowned, everything you say about Him must be true. I have decided He can take care of us, too."

The eyes of every Sawi in the manhouse fixed on Nair. Don felt no need to explain what had happened. Everyone could feel the loving Presence who had visited their leader. Some rubbed their elbows. Others squirmed nervously.

***

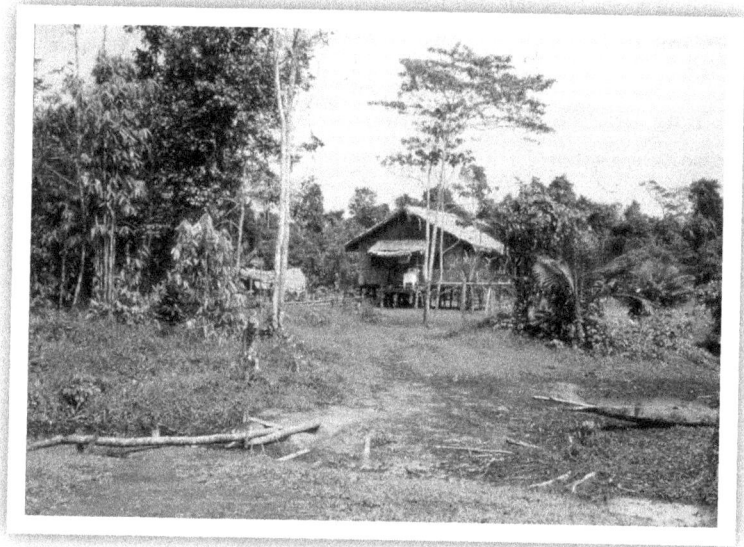

The Richardsons' home in Kamur

Within two weeks of Nair's decision nearly every member of his household had also decided to receive Jesus as their Peace Child. Many other important Sawi leaders also chose to follow Jesus, including Paha and Kani, Haenam's masters of treachery.

Others, however, made it clear that they rejected Christ in spite of the miracles of healing and power they witnessed.

"Let those believe who want to believe," they said. "We'll stay as we are."

***

Don and Carol lived among the Sawi for fifteen years. They had two more children, Paul and Valerie. Several evangelists from a tribal group in the highlands joined Don and Carol in ministering to the three thousand Sawi living in eighteen villages scattered across more than six hundred square miles of swamps. In time, other foreign missionaries also joined them. The Richardsons translated the New Testament into the Sawi language and taught the people how to read so that they could study the Bible for themselves. Sawi believers formed churches pastored by members of their own tribe.

CHAPTER 21

CHRISTMAS COMES TO THE KRONKEL

Narrow dugouts carrying fifty Mauro villagers materialized out of the heat-shimmer on the surface of the Kronkel. They approached warily. Many years had passed since Yae's murder and the waves of retaliatory killings, but the Mauro were still nervous about venturing so close to Haenam.

This was Christmas—the day chosen for the first large-scale Sawi intervillage feast in living memory. The flesh of five pigs sizzled over cooking fires. Young girls thrust sharp sticks through thousands of squirming beetle grubs and toasted them in the flames. Their mothers wrapped hundreds of slender sago loaves in *yohom* leaves for cooking. They struggled to make the day a joyous and festive one, but so many things seemed to get in the way—and the arrival of the Mauro villagers brought even more tension.

Alone and solemn, Kani the legendmaker stood watching them from the edge of Haenam. Sensing his inner turmoil, Don quietly stepped up behind him and laid his hand on Kani's shoulder. A soft morning breeze stirred the *kunai* grass around them.

"Kani," Don said gently, "After all these years, at last I have persuaded these men of Mauro to forget their hate and suspicion and come here to meet with you and your people on this ground. Now you…"

"Tuan!" Kani interrupted. "They are the very men who killed my brother. And they nearly killed me." He touched the ugly scar left on his back by a Mauro spear. Kani had not forgotten Mauro's treachery.

A pang of apprehension stabbed through Don. Had he misjudged the rightness of the moment? Perhaps Kani's newfound Christian faith was not yet strong enough to hold back his former violent ways in a moment of temptation. The men from Mauro were nearer now, trusting in the assurances Don had given them.

"Kani," he replied, laboring against the sudden dismay welling up inside him. "I see your wound, and I understand the even deeper wound within your memory. And I know what your forefathers taught you to do to men who have wronged you, as these men have wronged you.

"But your forefathers never knew what you and I know, Kani— that the perfect Peace Child has been given, and *still lives!* Because of that Peace Child God has forgiven you, my friend. And because of that Peace Child, you also must forgive the men of Mauro."

Don waited for an answer, but none came, even as the sound of Mauro's paddles reached the shore.

The Mauro dugouts swept past, heading for the mooring at the mouth of the tributary. Kani's eyes narrowed as he watched them.

Don turned away from Kani with sadness and walked over to welcome the guests. As he approached the Mauro, he noticed they were looking past him at Kani and the longhouses of Haenam. They, too, were remembering the fateful day when Yae, their ambassador for peace, had set out for Haenam and never returned. The words of Anai's dirge still echoed in their minds:

Oh who will deal with the children of treachery?
Oh what will it take to make them cease?

***

By mid-morning, several hundred Sawi from a half-dozen villages had beached their canoes near the Richardsons' home and joined in with the guests from Mauro, Haenam, and Kamur. Tension between the tribes crackled in the air. Many of the visitors refused to mingle with those from other villages. Instead, they pulled apart into small groups, watchful and apprehensive.

Don sensed violence throbbing through the village. Before it had a chance to erupt, a long Kayagar dugout appeared from upstream. A group of young men followed Don to the edge of the Kronkel to meet it. Lying in the boat was Hurip, the Kayagar man who had shown the first steel axe to the men of Haenam years before. He was suffering from pneumonia, gasping for breath as Don knelt beside his dugout and felt for his pulse.

Before he had finished counting Hurip's pulse a voice—ominous and edged with bitterness—spoke from behind Don. "Tuan, you won't give medicine to that man, will you?"

Don recognized the voice of Amio, Nair's son. Looking over his shoulder, Don saw that Amio's slim, brown body was trembling with emotion.

"You want Hurip to die?" he asked in surprise.

"Yes," Amio hissed.

Anxiously Don rose and faced him. He was glad that Amio was unarmed, but one word would bring his friends running with weapons. Hurip's Kayagar friends, meanwhile, gripped their spear-paddles tightly. They sensed trouble, even though they could not understand the Sawi conversation.

"Why?" Don asked.

Amio's voice choked with emotion as he replied: "Remember I told you my father once gave a peace child to the Kayagar, only to learn later that they had killed the baby and devoured it?"

Don nodded and Amio continued, "The man lying in this canoe is the man my father gave that child to. He is the man who killed and butchered my little brother!"

Now Don trembled too. First Kani, and now Amio. Could the Sawi really forgive their enemies for Christ's sake? Somehow, sometime, they must forgive, but perhaps it was too soon...

For a moment Don stood speechless before Amio, praying for wisdom. Then an old memory stirred. Reaching out with both hands, Don gripped Amio by his earlobes. The Sawi warrior was startled, but he did not draw away. He listened intently while Don said, "I plead the Peace Child!"

Amio shot back, "The peace child my father gave to Hurip is dead! Hurip himself killed him!"

"But the Peace Child God gave still lives!" Don countered. "And because He lives, you may not take vengeance against Hurip. Forgive him, Amio, for Jesus' sake!"

Don still gripped Amio's ears.

The conflict on the young man's face raged to an almost overwhelming intensity, and then began to subside. Soon it gave way to a glow of new understanding. Eventually Amio looked down with gentleness on his dying enemy.

Don released Amio's earlobes and said as matter-of-factly as he could, "Amio, I need help to carry Hurip to the medical house."

With deep resolve, Amio squared his shoulders and said, "Tuan, let me carry Hurip alone!"

Two Kayagar lifted Hurip onto Amio's back and watched in awe as the young man bore his semi-conscious burden toward the clinic. Following behind Amio, Don noticed someone else who had observed Amio's change of heart—Kani. As Don passed by, Kani gave him a look that assured him he no longer had any reason to fear his intentions regarding the visitors from Mauro.

Almost dizzy with gladness, Don breathed a deep sigh of relief. It was beginning to feel like Christmas Day after all!

***

After Amio had settled Hurip at the clinic, Don and Carol walked together along a path toward the thatch-roofed church where the feast was now ready. Sawi Christians mingled with groups of still-reluctant guests who preferred to stay close to their spear-paddles and canoes.

One by one, bands of solemn strangers yielded to the kindly persuasion of the believers and began to file toward the church. Wide-eyed and wondering, they stepped under festive palm branches and entered the cool, spacious interior. Their skin tingled with the new feeling of unreserved welcome that seemed to charge the very air.

Don, Carol, Stephen, and Shannon watched together as Christian Sawi from many different villages rose and crossed the now-crowded meeting house to lay gifts of sago, beetle grubs, and wild pork at the feet of former enemies. While the giving went on and on, the full-throated singing of Sawi Christmas carols swelled around them, thanking God for giving His Son, the greatest gift of all.

Next Isai, a Sawi preacher, rose to his feet and read the verse of Scripture that Don had shared when he introduced Jesus as God's Peace Child: "For unto us a Child is born; unto us a Son is given…"

Don looked around at the radiant faces of believers filled with adoration of the Peace Child, Immanuel, God with us. God's good news of great joy for all people had finally reached the Sawi.

Ten years after the Richardsons arrived, the Sawi built a circular church building known as the "Sawidome", which seated 1,000 worshipers.

EPILOGUE

Intertribal warfare became nothing but a painful memory in the swamps surrounding Kamur. Sawi, Kayagar, Auyu, Asmat, and Atohwaem villagers mingled freely around the Christian medical clinic's door. They called themselves "the Five Tribes" and formed a partnership to take the gospel to yet other groups hidden in the jungle.

The Richardson family lived among them for 15 years. During this time, Shannon, Paul and Valerie were born and grew up in the jungle on the banks of the Kronkel. In time, more missionary families joined them—both from Western countries and from other parts of Indonesia. The Sawi culture successfully leaped from the Stone Age to the twentieth century within one generation because the gospel of Jesus Christ enabled them to live at peace with one another as part of the modern world. Today, the Sawi church continues to grow in strength and numbers, always remembering their heritage and God's gift of the eternal Peace Child.

If you want to hear how life is different for the Sawi today because of the gospel, visit *Pioneers.org/NevertheSame* to watch *Never the Same,* a short video filmed fifty years after Don and Carol witnessed the exchange of the Sawi peace children. You'll meet Don, Stephen, Shannon, Paul, and many Sawi and Kayagar tribespeople whose lives God impacted through the Richardson family.

And what about you? How have you responded to God's Peace Child? Have you accepted Jesus' payment for your sins and entered into peace with God? He is waiting. So are many other villages and tribes and peoples who have never heard the story of Jesus' birth, death, and resurrection. They don't know that they can have peace with God through the gift of His Son. Will you be the one to tell them?

In 2012, Don Richardson returned to Kamur with his three sons, Stephen, Shannon, and Paul, for a reunion to celebrate 50 years of the gospel's work among the Sawi.

DISCUSSION QUESTIONS

1. What do you think of the way the Sawi tribe lived, and why do you think they had those practices and beliefs?

2. How do you think the arrival of the gospel influenced the culture of the Sawi?

3. Don says that God was excited about what He was going to do among the Sawi through the Richardsons. Do you agree? What else do you think God gets excited about? Do you feel excited when you think about cross-cultural missions?

4. Do you agree with Don's conclusion that the Sawi were more spiritually needy than the Kayagar because they did not yet have anyone who could explain the gospel in their language? How does your answer influence how you think about the lost in the world today? Is everyone's spiritual need equal?

5. Do you think Amio was right to forgive Hurip for killing his little brother? Should Hurip be punished?

6. When the Sawi first heard the story of Jesus, they saw Judas as the hero based on their cultural values (they admired Judas' betrayal). Do you think that American values ever cause us to misunderstand stories in the Bible?

7. What do you think would have happened if Don and Carol had kept on presenting the gospel in their normal way, without using the metaphor of the Peace Child?

8. Can you think of any such metaphors in the Bible from Jewish culture (for example, the Lamb of God, living water, etc.)?

9. Do you believe that God can forgive someone who lies and murders like Kani and Nair? Does that mean that God doesn't care about the wrong they did? What offenses do you find hardest to forgive?

10. Do you think that Don and Carol could have had this kind of influence on the Sawi if they had only visited for brief periods and worked through a translator like Hadi, rather than learning the language and staying for many years?

11. Very few tribes today remain as isolated as the Sawi were in the 1950s. However, hundreds of people groups still have no one to share the gospel in their own language and culture. Some live in remote jungles far away. Others are refugees in big cities in America and other countries around the world. How do you think that taking the gospel to them today would be different than what the Richardsons experienced?

12. What characteristics or preparation do you think helped Don and Carol be effective missionaries among the Sawi? Can you imagine yourself doing something similar? How would you need to change, and what would you need to learn?

13. You read about how the McCains helped the Richardsons begin their ministry among the Sawi and how evangelists from another tribe joined them later on. Other people, who are not named in this book, also contributed to the work among the Sawi. Most missionaries today do not work by themselves. What would you look for in a teammate to help you take the gospel to an unreached people group? What help do you think you would need?

14. What do you think would have been the most fun about growing up in a place like Kamur, as the Richardson children did? What do you think would be the hardest? How do you think they would be different from you and your friends?

15. Do you sense that God has been saying anything to you personally as you have read the Richardson's story? How do you think your life may be affected?

ABOUT THE AUTHORS

In 1962, Don Richardson and his wife, Carol, embarked on a missionary career in Netherlands New Guinea (now Papua, Indonesia), where they served for 15 years among the Sawi. Don and Carol designed an alphabet suited to their language, taught the Sawi to read, and translated the New Testament into their native tongue. As a registered nurse, Carol was known as "the woman who makes everyone well." Following their time in Indonesia, Don wrote books and spoke at churches, conferences, and Perspectives classes, mobilizing many to pursue missions. Among his most well-known books are *Peace Child* (from which *Treachery on the Twisted River* is adapted), *Eternity in Their Hearts,* and *Lords of the Earth.* Don passed away in 2018 at the age of 83 after a battle with brain cancer.

***

Karen Robertson retired recently from a career of teaching elementary school, augmented by raising two children with her school-teacher husband, John. The Robertsons savor good books that they frequently share with their own children or students in class. After several years of teaching in California public schools, John and Karen relocated to Indonesia and then Malaysia to teach in Christian international schools for 12 years. The Robertsons currently reside in Santa Barbara, California. Karen has written and created abundant classroom and Sunday school materials.

www.ingramcontent.com/pod-product-compliance
Lightning Source LLC
LaVergne TN
LVHW041252080426
835510LV00009B/698